RECORDED VERSIONS GUITAR

AUTHENTIC TRANSCRIPTIONS
WITH NOTES AND TABLATURE

**Transcribed by
PETE BILLMANN
and
JEFF CATANIA**

GOO GOO
a boy named goo

Cover photo © VANCE GELLERT/SWANSTOCK
Used by Permission.

ISBN 0-7935-6408-5

HAL•LEONARD® CORPORATION
7777 W. BLUEMOUND RD. P.O. BOX 13819 MILWAUKEE, WI 53213

Photo by Frank Ockenfels
Courtesy of Warner Bros. Records

Photo by Anthony Stroppa

Photo by Jeffrey Mayer

Photo by Jeffrey Mayer

Long Way Down

Words and Music by John Rzeznik

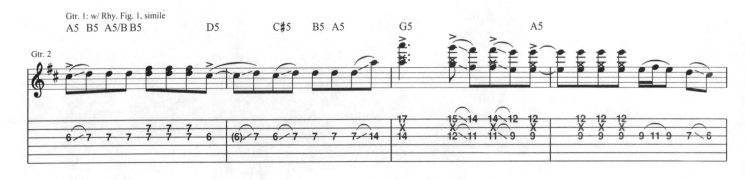

Touch me now ___ and I ___ don't care. ___ When ___ you take ___
Is ___ there an - y - thing ___ to feel? ___ Is ___ it pain ___
Take an oth - er piece ___ of me. ___ Give my mind ___

simile on repeats

___ me I'm ___ not there? ___ Al - most hu - man ___ but I'll
___ that makes ___ you real? ___ Cut me off ___ be - fore it kills ___
___ a new ___ dis ease and the black ___ and white ___ world

Chorus

Gtr. 1: w/ Rhy. Fill 1, 3rd time   Gtr. 1: w/ Rhy. Fig. 1, 2 times, simile

nev - er be ___ the same. ___
___ me.
nev - er fades ___ to gray. ___

(Long way ___ down. _____)

Gtr. 3

Rhy. Fill 1
Gtr. 1

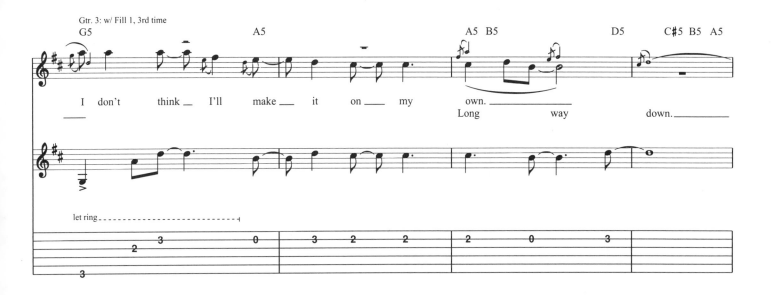

I don't think __ I'll make __ it on __ my own. __
Long way down. __

I don't wan - na live __ in here __ a - lone.
Long way __ down. __

9

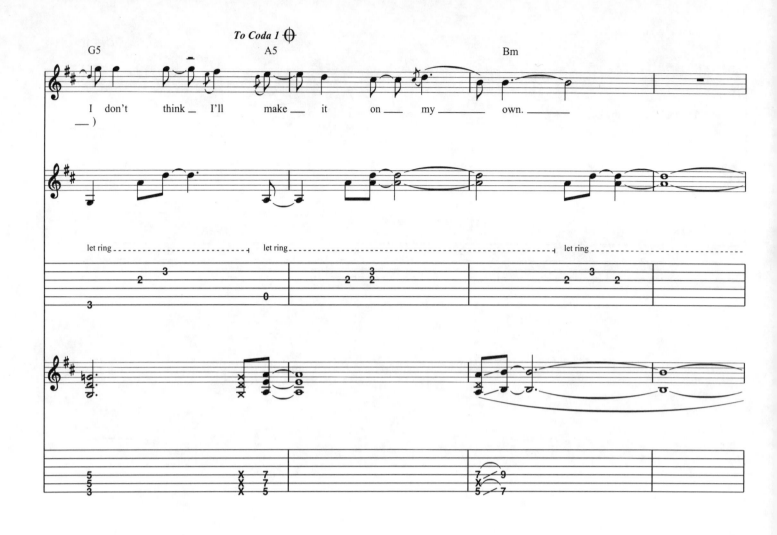

I don't think I'll make it on my own.

_( )_

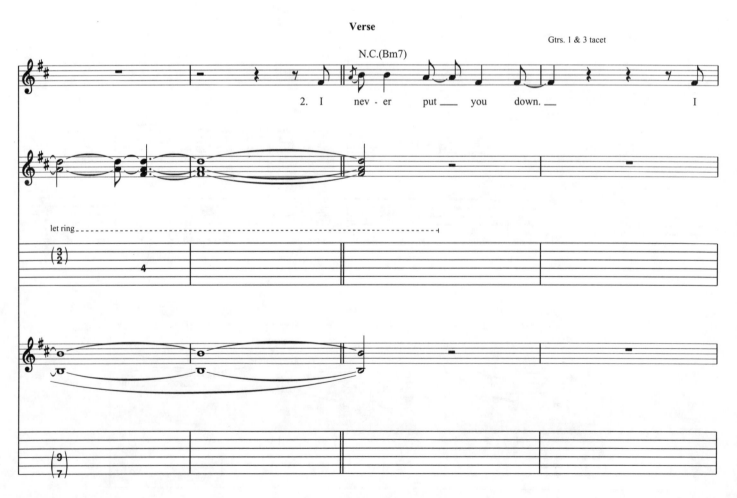

Verse

Gtrs. 1 & 3 tacet

2. I nev-er put you down. I

⊕ Coda 1

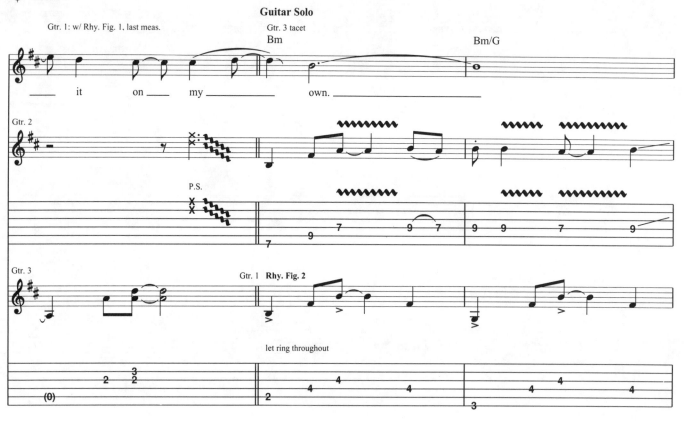

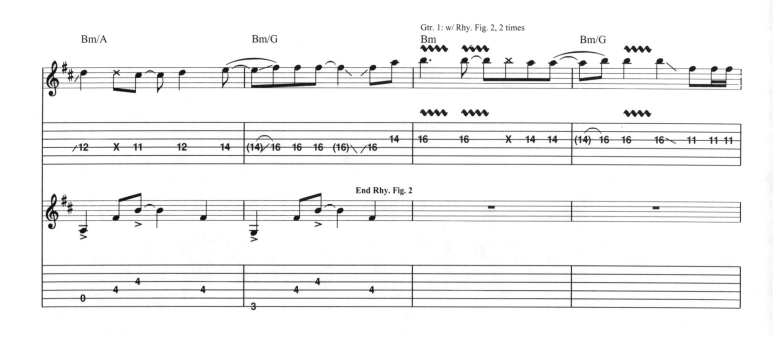

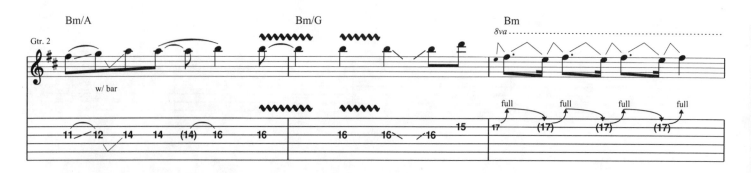

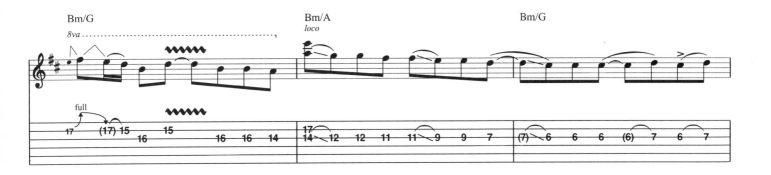

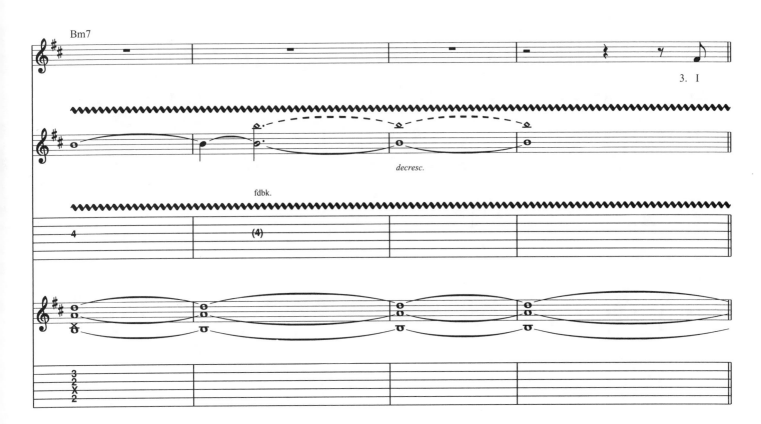

Verse

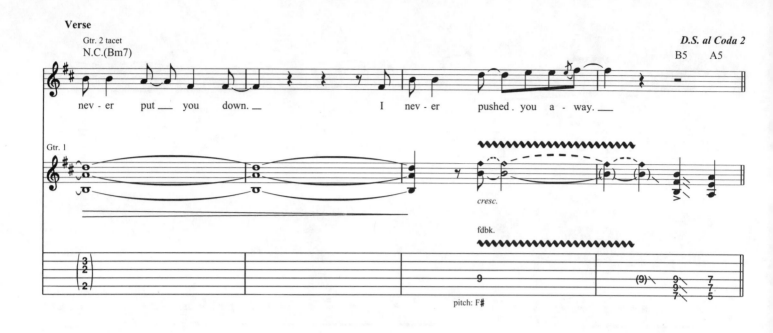

Gtr. 2 tacet
N.C.(Bm7)

B5   A5

never put you down. I never pushed you away.

cresc.

fdbk.

pitch: F#

⊕ Coda 2

Gtr. 1: w/ Rhy. Fig. 1, last 2 meas.
G5   A5

Gtr. 3: w/ Rhy. Fig. 3, 4 times
G5   A5

I don't think I'll make it on my own,

Gtr. 3   **Rhy. Fig. 3**   **End Rhy. Fig. 3**   **Rhy. Fig. 4**
Gtr. 1

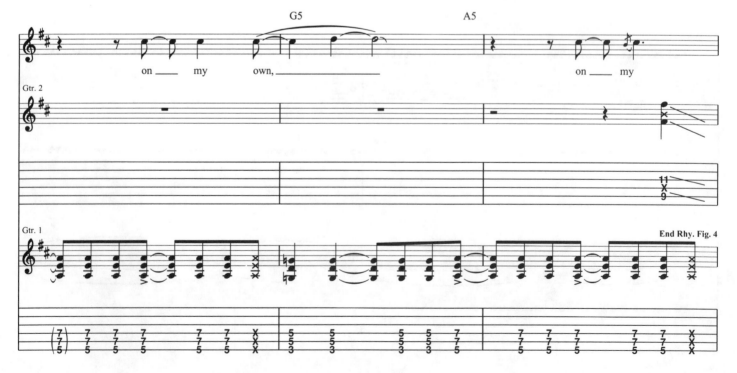

G5   A5

on my own, on my

Gtr. 2

Gtr. 1   **End Rhy. Fig. 4**

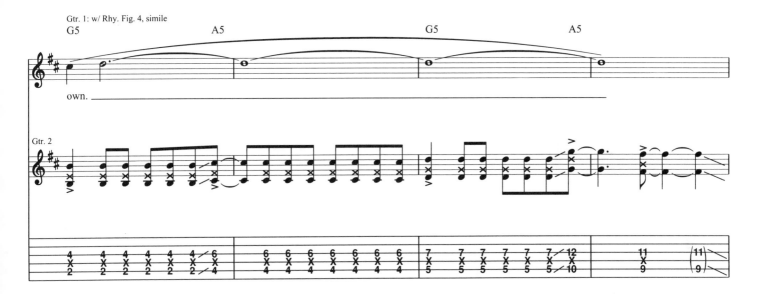

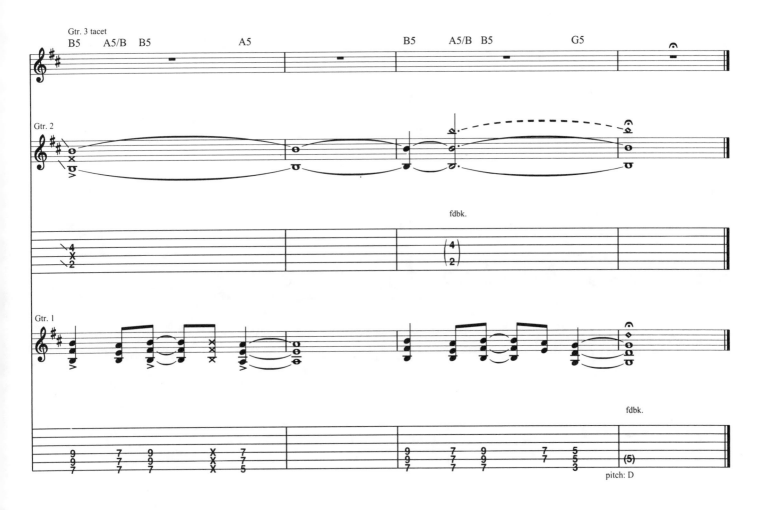

Burnin' Up

Words and Music by Goo Goo Dolls

Interlude

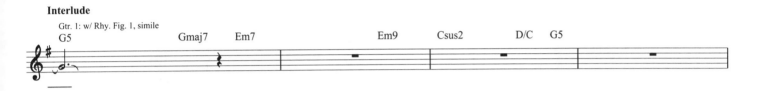

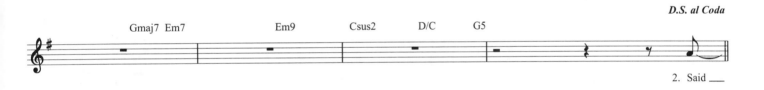

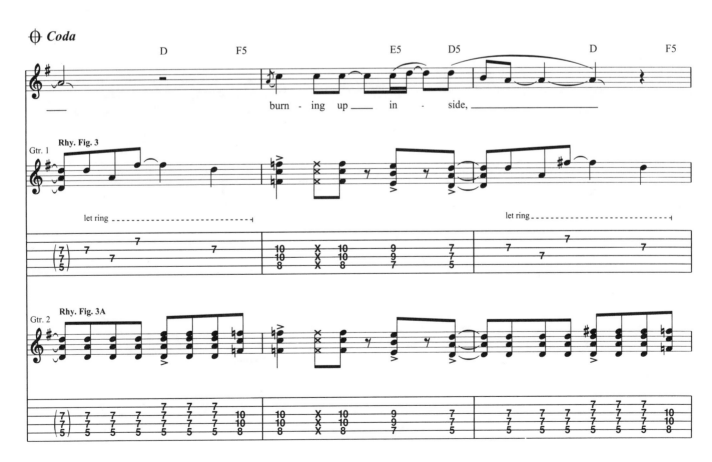

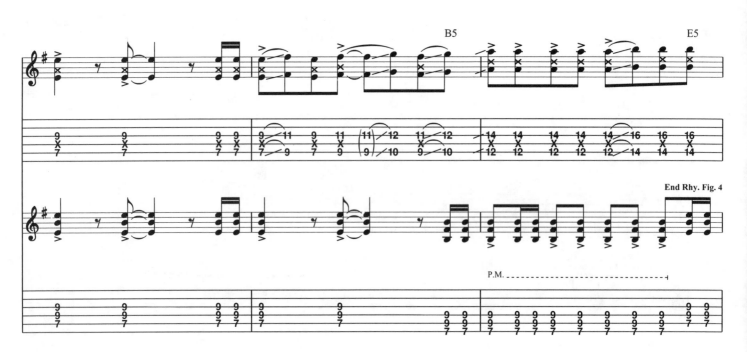

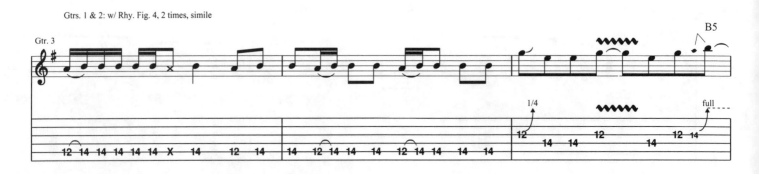

18

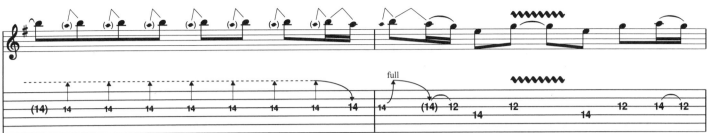
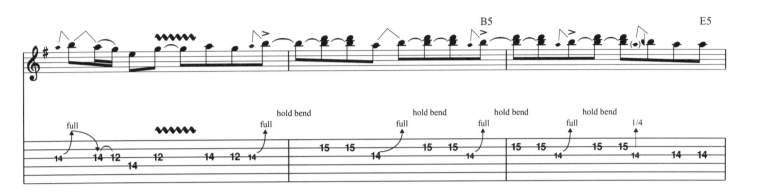
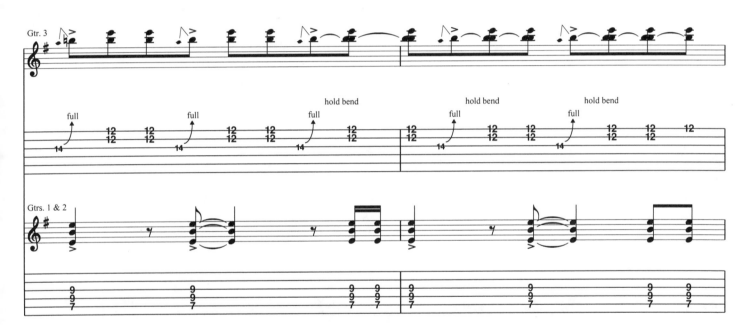
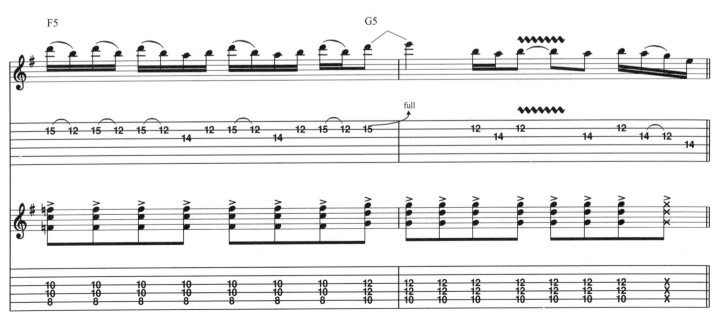

Verse

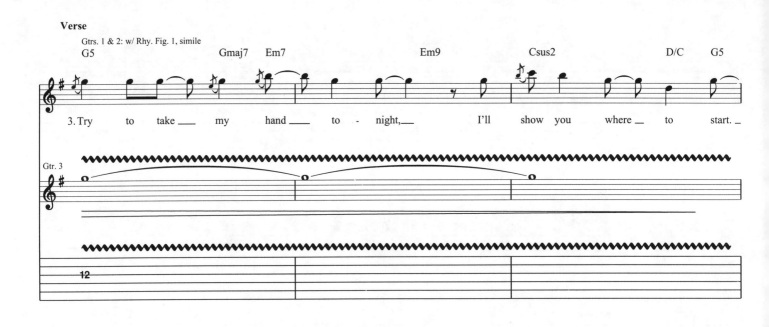

Gtrs. 1 & 2: w/ Rhy. Fig. 1, simile

G5   Gmaj7 Em7   Em9   Csus2   D/C   G5

3. Try to take my hand to - night, I'll show you where to start.

Gtr. 3

12

Gtr. 3 tacet

Gmaj7 Em7   Em9   Csus2   D/C   G5

'Cause ev - 'ry word that left your lips is like a nee - dle through my heart.

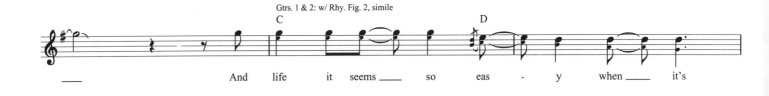

Gtrs. 1 & 2: w/ Rhy. Fig. 2, simile

C   D

And life it seems so eas - y when it's

Gtrs. 1 & 2:
w/ Rhy. Figs. 3 & 3A, simile

G   E5   F5   E5 D5   D F5

from my eas - y chair and you're burn - in' up in - side,

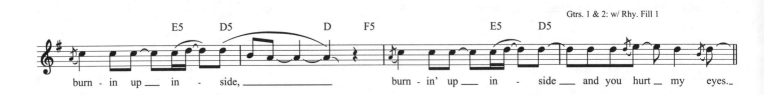

Gtrs. 1 & 2: w/ Rhy. Fill 1

E5   D5   D   F5   E5   D5

burn - in up in - side, burn - in' up in - side and you hurt my eyes.

Outro

Gtrs. 1 & 2: w/ Rhy. Fig. 1, 1st 7 meas.

G5 Gmaj7 Em7   Em9   Csus2   D/C   G5   Gmaj7 Em7

('Cause you're burn - in' up in - side.   Hurt my eyes,

'Cause you're burn - in' up ___ in - side. ___ hurt ___ my eyes, ___

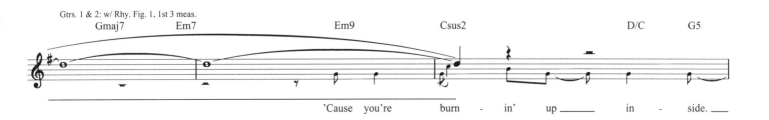

'Cause you're burn - in' up ___ in - side. ___

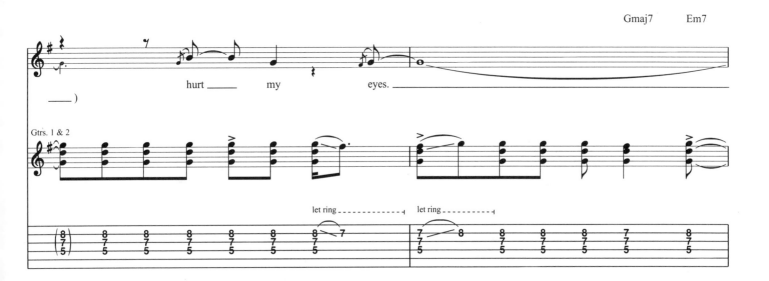

hurt ___ my eyes.

Gtrs. 1 & 2

let ring ___ let ring ___

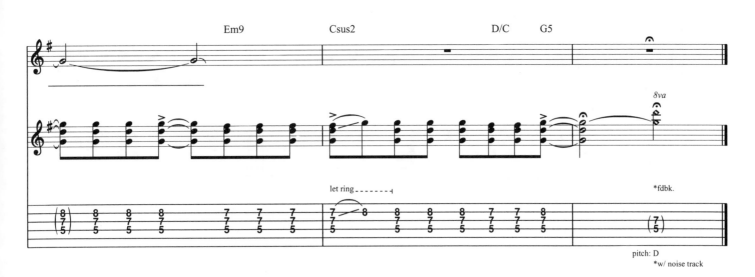

let ring ___

pitch: D
*w/ noise track

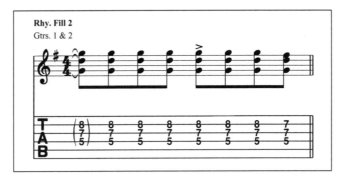

Rhy. Fill 2
Gtrs. 1 & 2

Naked

Words and Music by John Rzeznik

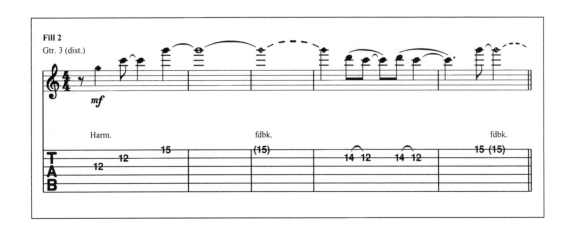

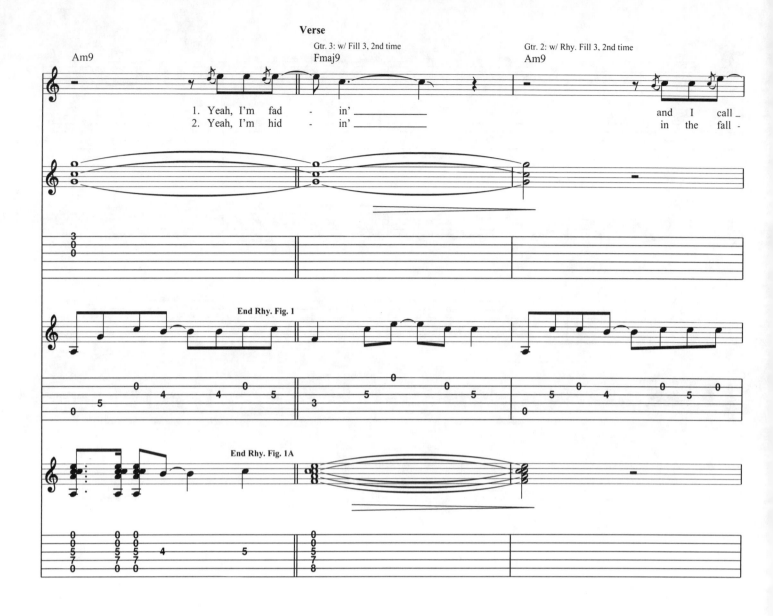

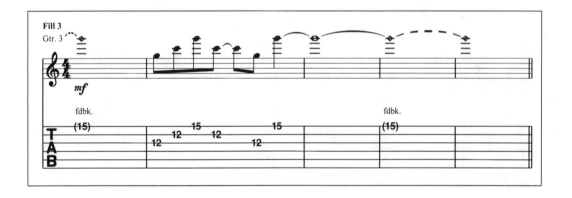

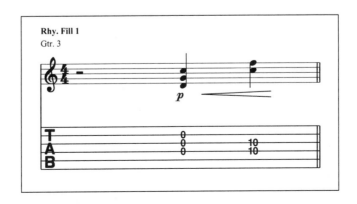

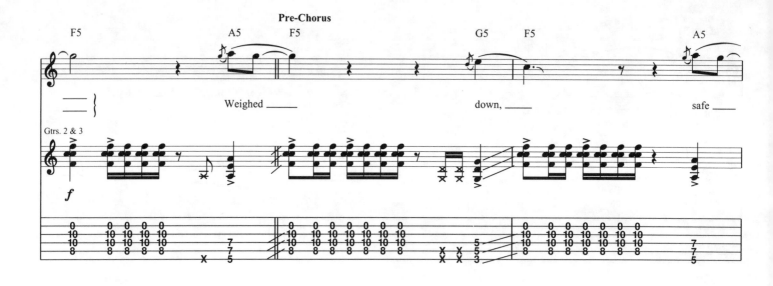

* Chord symbols reflect implied tonality.

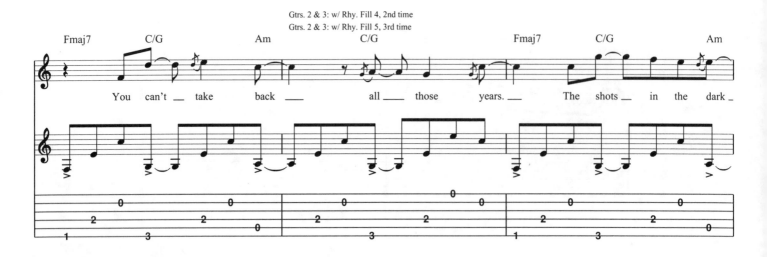

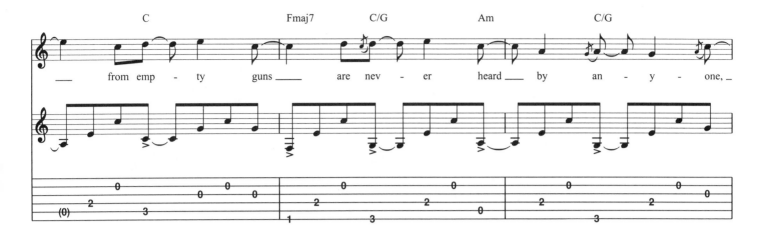

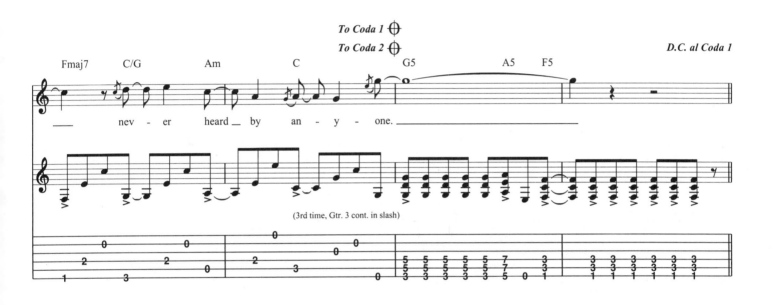

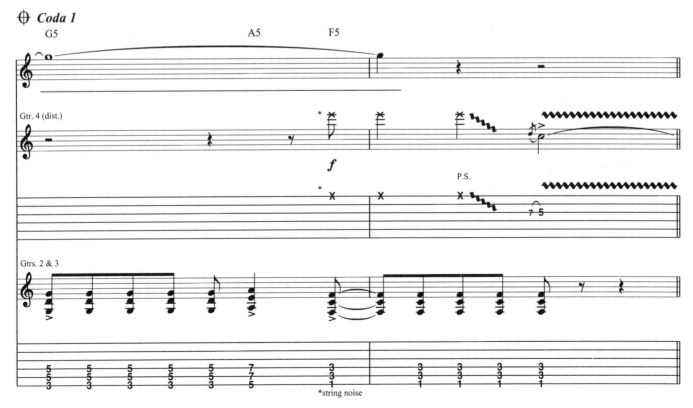

Gtrs. 2 & 3: w/ Rhy. Figs. 1 & 1A, 2 times, simile

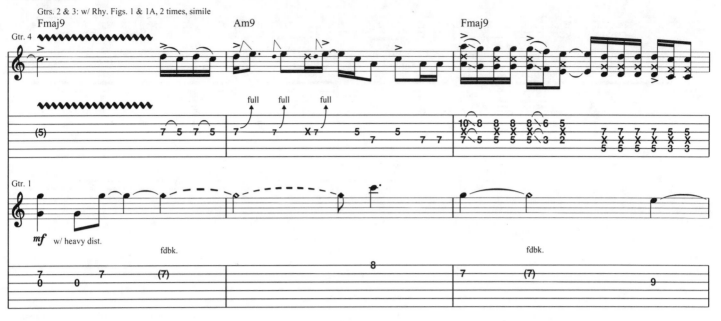

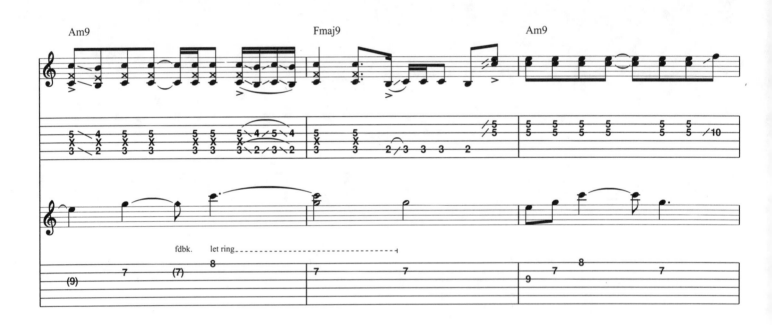

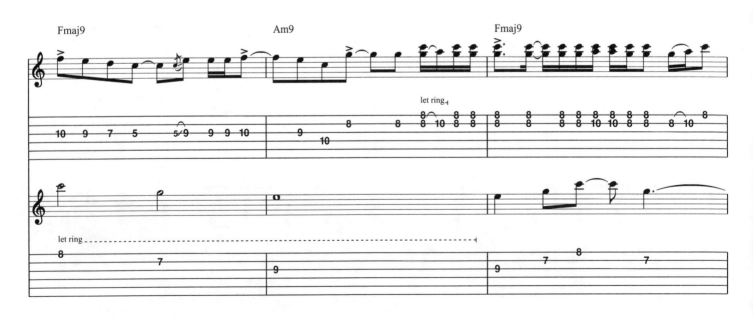

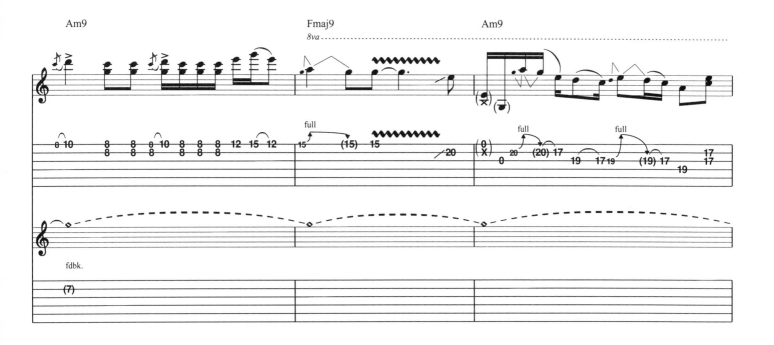

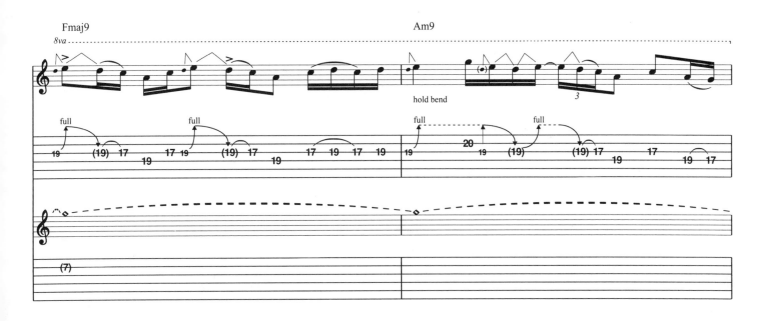

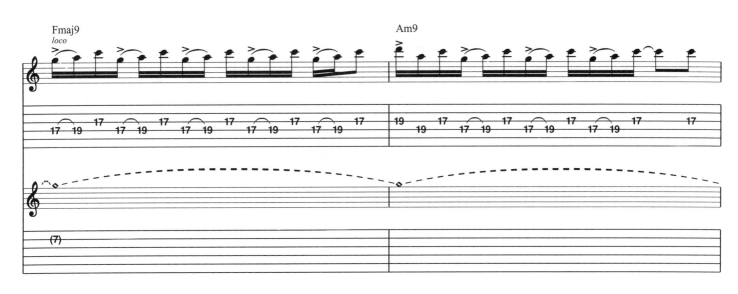

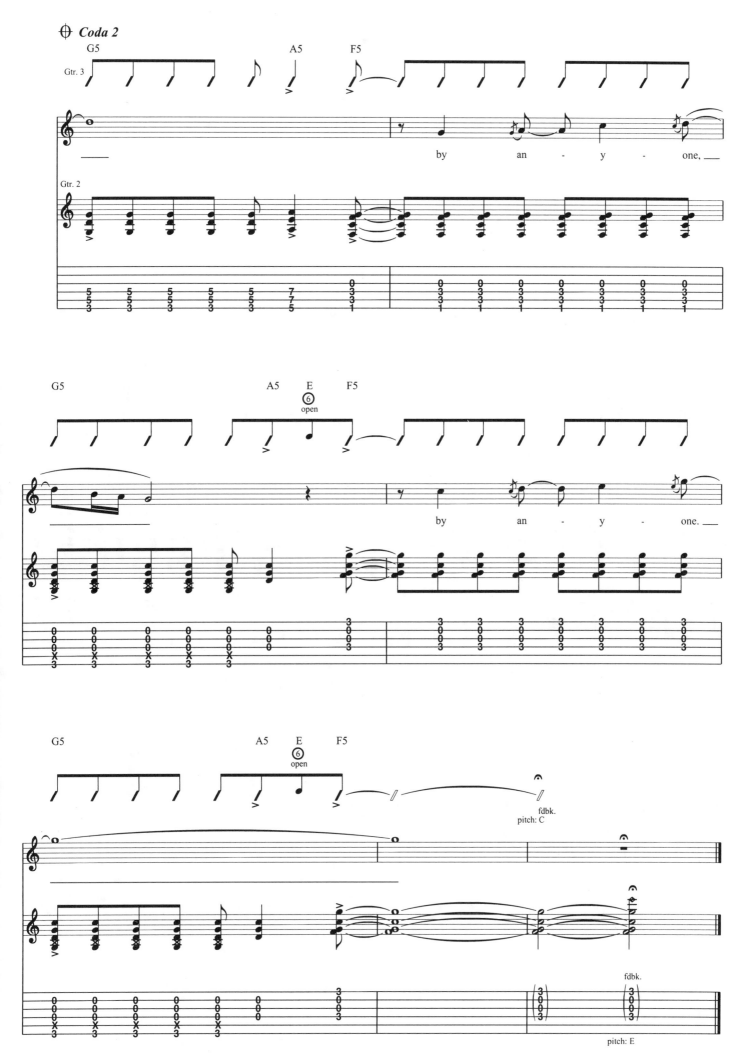

by an - y - one, ___

by an - y - one. ___

Flat Top

Words and Music by John Rzeznik

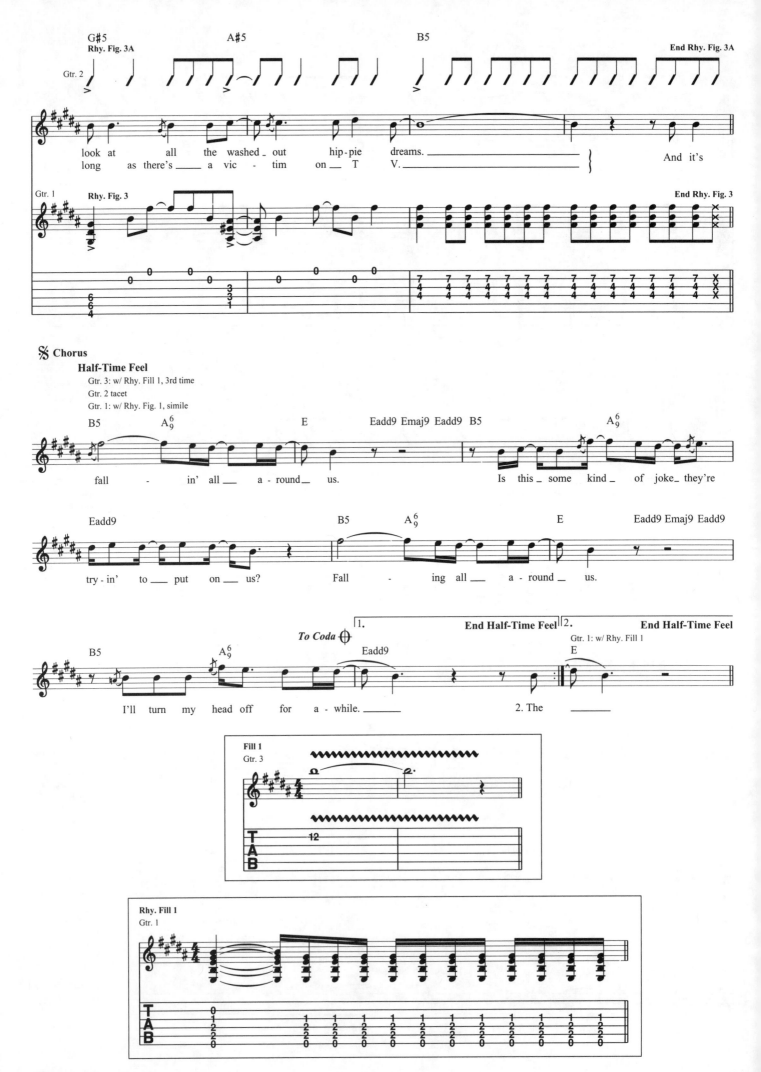

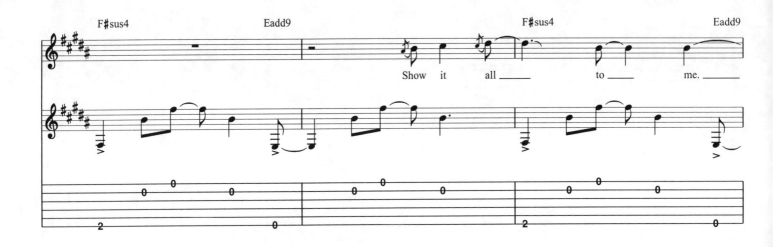

Show it all ___ to ___ me. ___

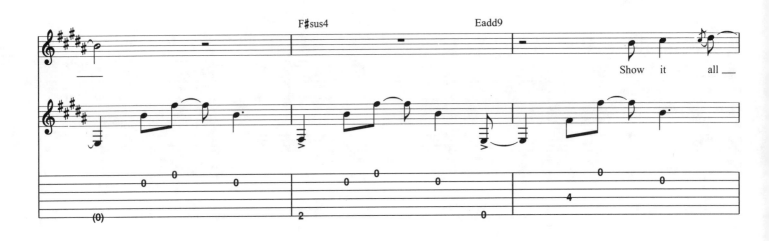

Show it all ___

Guitar Solo
Half-Time Feel
Gtr. 2 tacet
Gtr. 1: w/ Rhy. Fig. 1

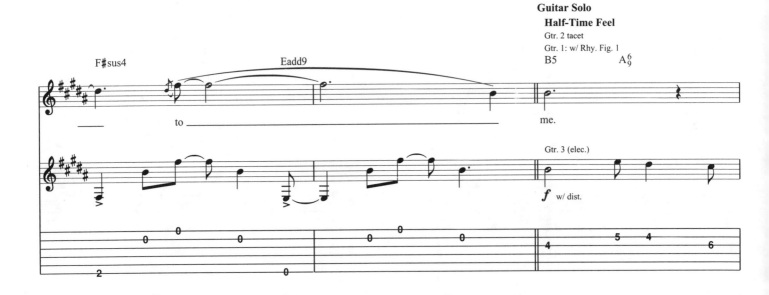

to ___ me.

Gtr. 3 (elec.)
f w/ dist.

End Half-Time Feel

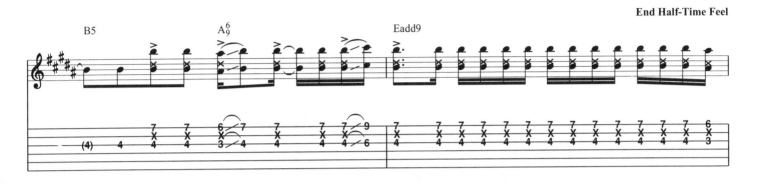

Gtrs. 1 & 2: w/ Rhy. Figs. 2 & 2A, 1 1/2 times, simile

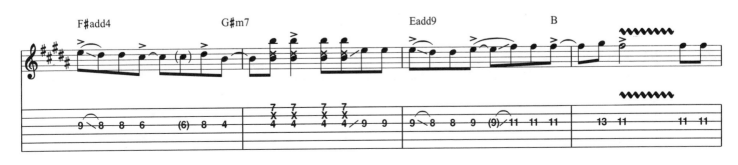

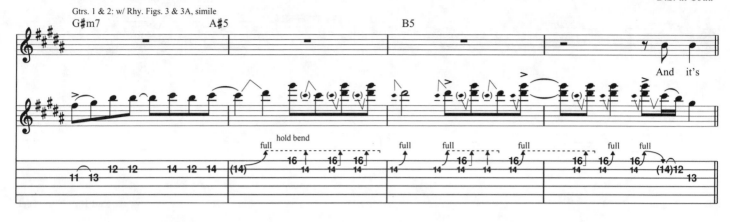

⊕ *Coda*

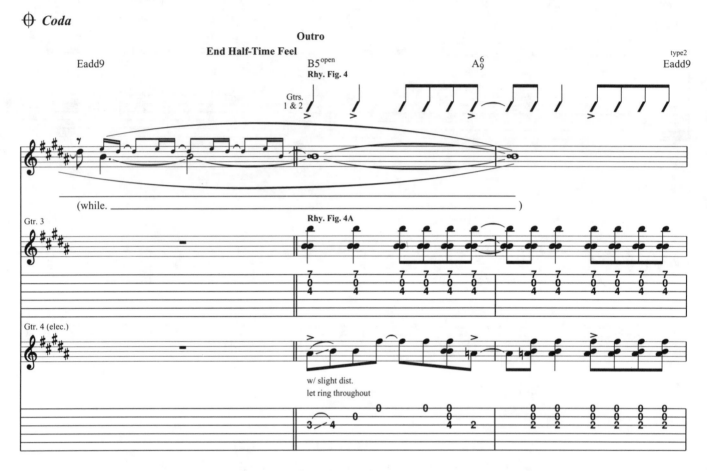

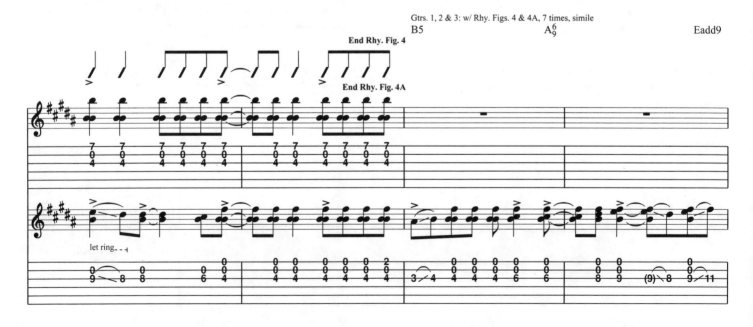

Impersonality

Words and Music by Goo Goo Dolls

*Chord symbols reflect overall tonality.
**doubled throughout

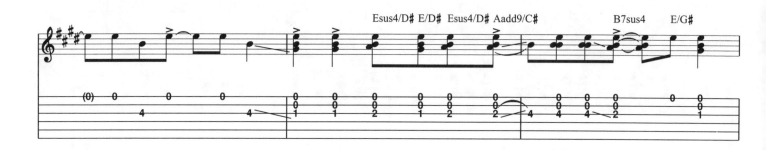

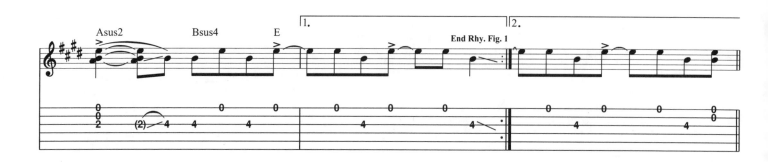

1. When I was three feet tall ___ I loved 'em all ___ and lived life for ___ my -

self. Fall - ing down ___ for laughs, ___ your pho - to - graph, ___ some pup - pets made ___ of ___

felt. Watch - ing life ___ in Oz, ___ Thanks - giv - ing eve ___ on Grand- ma's old ___ T V. ___

___ Danc - ing round ___ a - bout ___ I'd twist and shout ___ for ev' - ry - one ___ to see. ___

Chorus

Im - per - son - al - i - ty. ___

It's lean - in' hard ___ on me. ___

Fill 1
Gtr. 1

*Microphonic fdbk., not caused by string vibration.

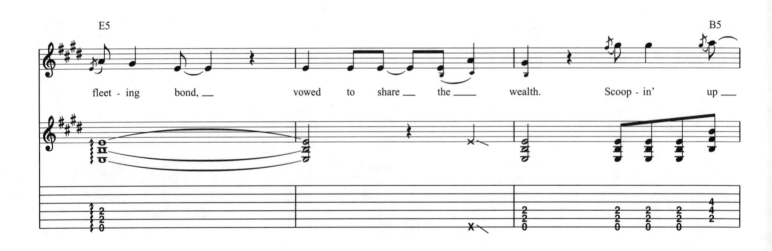

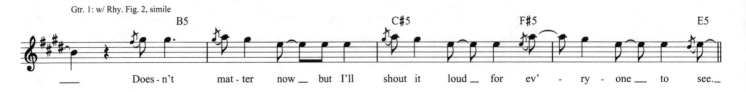

Guitar Solo

Name

Words and Music by John Rzeznik

Tuning:
① = E   ④ = E
② = E   ⑤ = A
③ = A   ⑥ = D

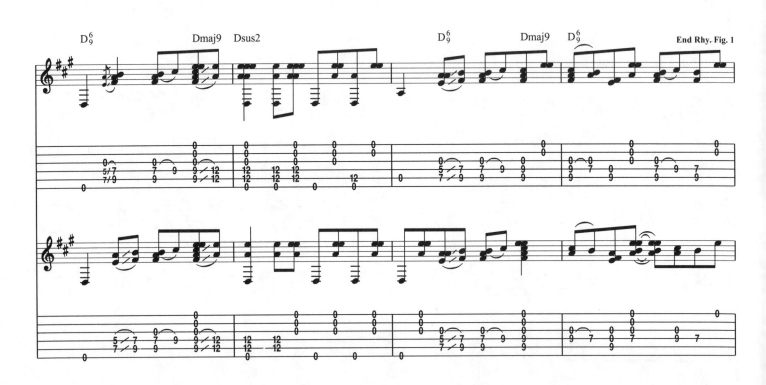

47

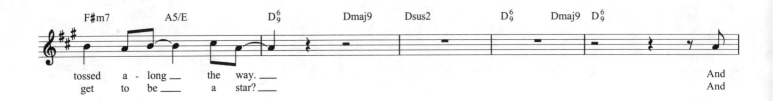

tossed a - long ___ the way. ___ And
get to be ___ a star? ___ And

let - ters that ___ you nev - er meant ___ to send, ___ get
don't it make ___ you sad ___ to know ___ that life ___ is

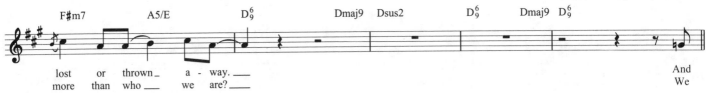

lost or thrown ___ a - way. ___ And
more than who ___ we are? ___ We

Chorus

now we're grown _ up or - phans ___ that nev - er knew _ their names. ___ We
grew up way _ too fast ___ and now there's noth-in' to ___ be - lieve. ___

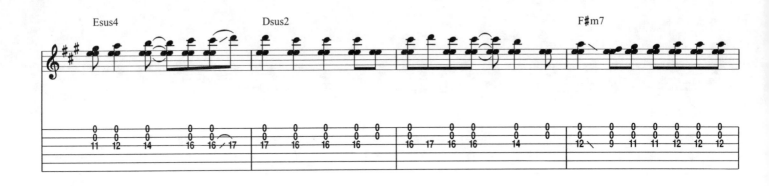

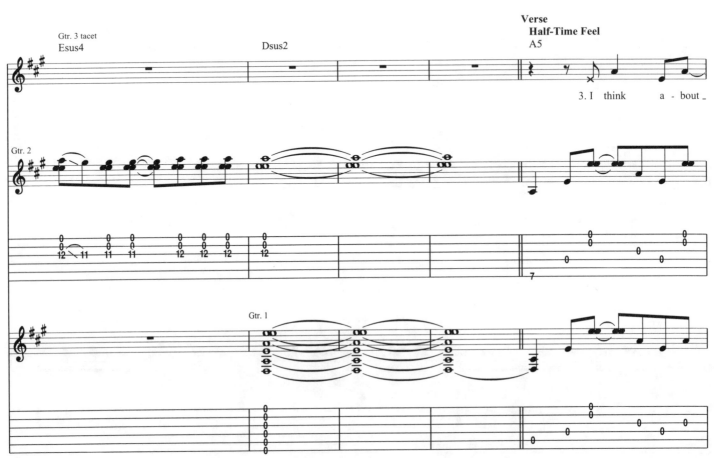

52

Only One

Words and Music by John Rzeznik

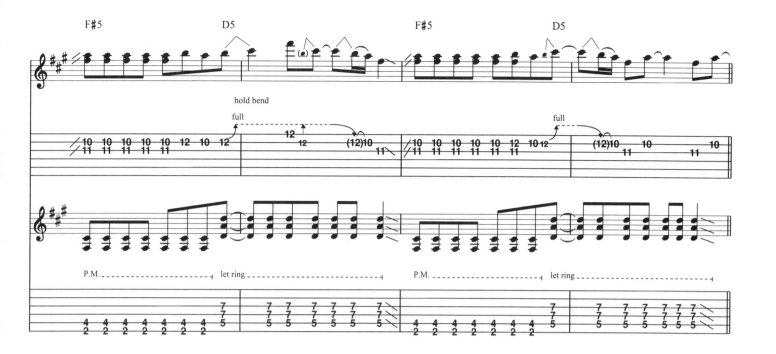

Chorus

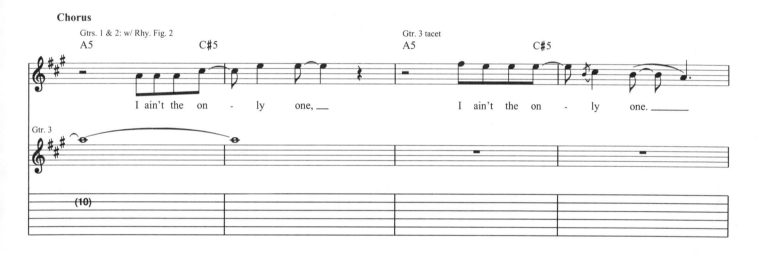

Gtrs. 1 & 2: w/ Rhy. Fig. 2

I ain't the on - ly one, ___ I ain't the on - ly one. _____

Gtr. 3

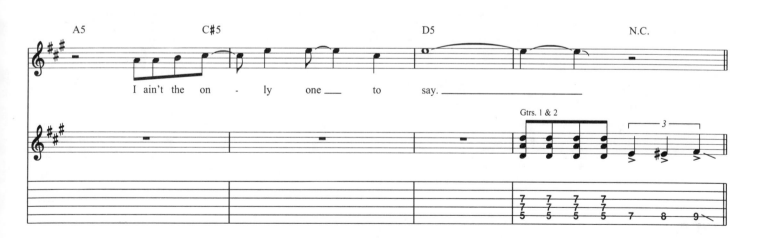

I ain't the on - ly one ___ to say. _____

Bridge

Gtrs. 1 & 2: w/ Riffs B & B1, 3 times
Gtr. 3: w/ Rhy. Fig. 3, 3 times

C#5

End Rhy. Fig. 3

Lit - tle pic - tures in __ my head __ are turn - in' in -

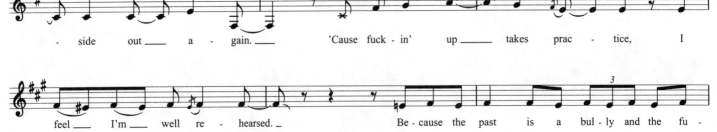

- side out __ a - gain. __ 'Cause fuck - in' up __ takes prac - tice, I

feel __ I'm __ well re - hearsed. __ Be - cause the past is a bul - ly and the fu -

ture's e - ven worse, you tell me what you fear ___ 'cause I can feel it like a curse. ___

Guitar Solo

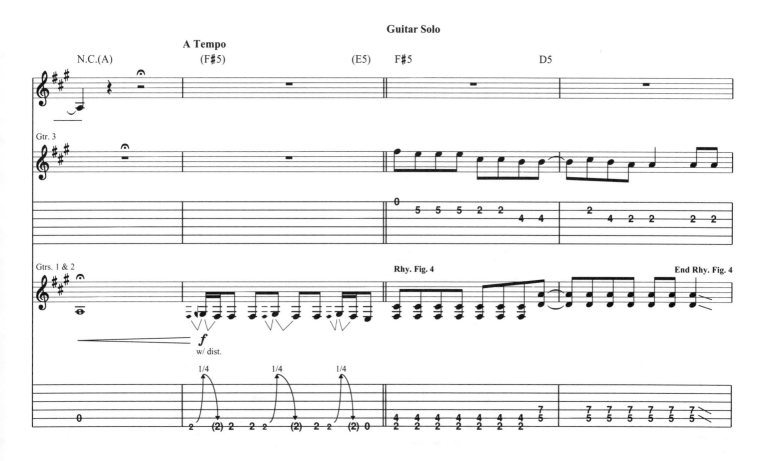

Verse

3. Well, you used to be a folk sing-er, now you're just a joke sing-er.

(cont. in slash)

D.S. al Coda

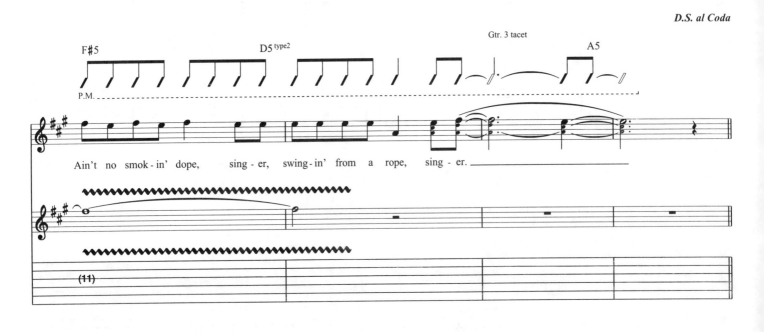

Gtr. 3 tacet

Ain't no smok-in' dope, sing-er, swing-in' from a rope, sing-er.

⊕ Coda

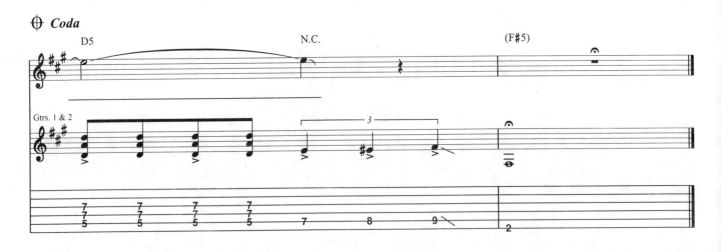

Somethin' Bad

Words and Music by Goo Goo Dolls

Gtr. 2: w/ Fill 1, 3rd time

not like me to feel __ so __ im-por-tant, __   And it's

not like me to go and wreck __ your day. __   And I

nev-er thought _ I'd see it so __ ex - ploi - ted. __   Ah, but I

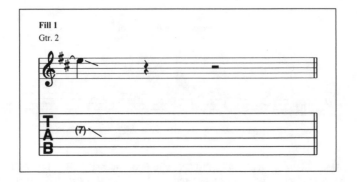

Fill 1
Gtr. 2

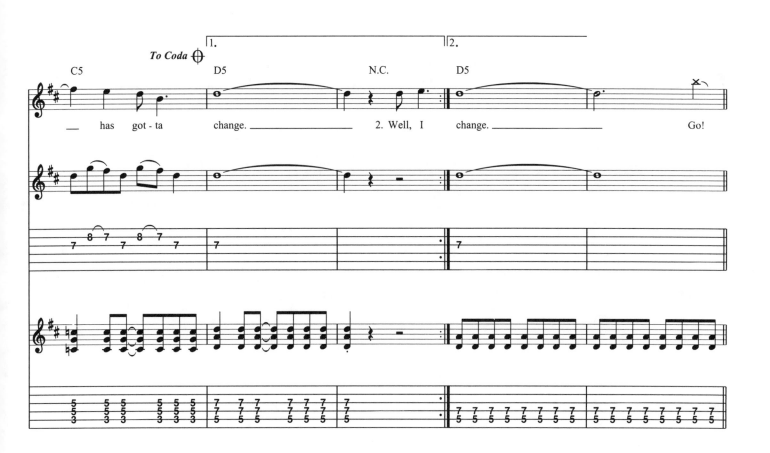

Guitar Solo

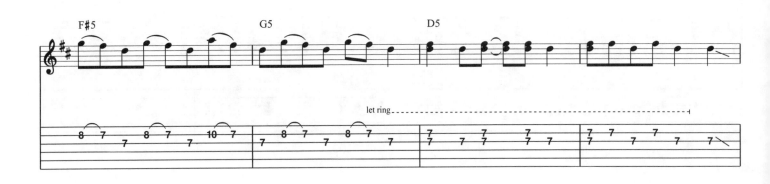

64

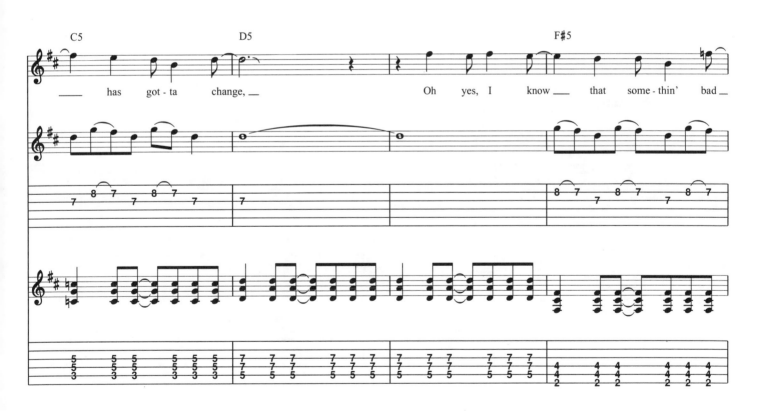

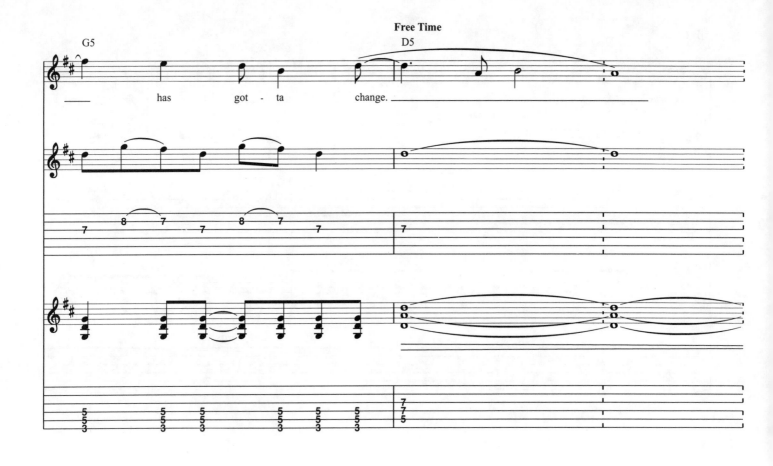

has got - ta change.

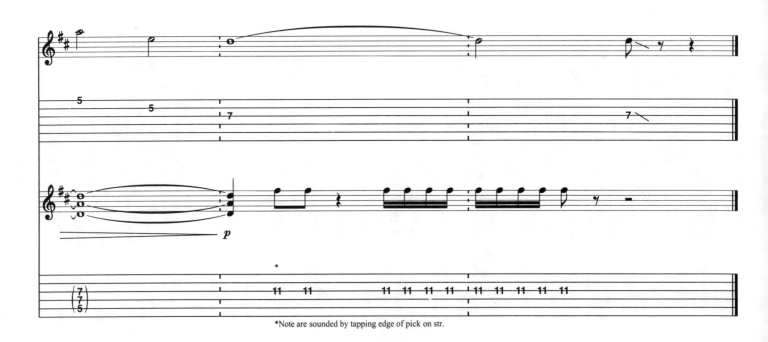

*Note are sounded by tapping edge of pick on str.

Ain't That Unusual

Words and Music by John Rzeznik

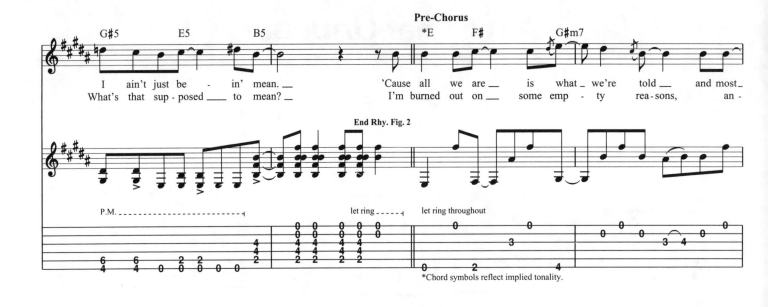

Pre-Chorus

*Chord symbols reflect implied tonality.

I ain't just be - in' mean. ___ 'Cause all we are ___ is what we're told ___ and most ___
What's that sup - posed ___ to mean? ___ I'm burned out on ___ some emp - ty rea - sons, an -

___ of that's been lies. ___ It's like a made ___ for T ___ V mov - ie and
oth - er waste of time. ___ There's some - thin' that ___ I wish ___ I'd said ___ but I ___

𝄋 Chorus

I just blew my line. ___ Some - day ___ you nev - er made ___ it,
___ don't think ___ it'd rhyme. ___ (Some - day ___

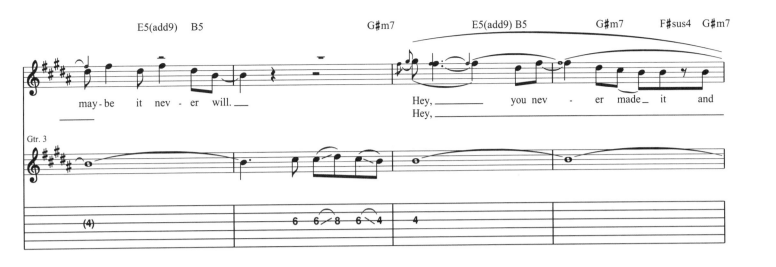

may - be it nev - er will. _____ Hey, _____ you nev - er made __ it and
Hey, _____

To Coda $\oplus$ **Verse**

ain't that un - us - u - al? ___ 2. Now I
___) 3. See, I'd love to be __ you, then at least then I'd see __ you.

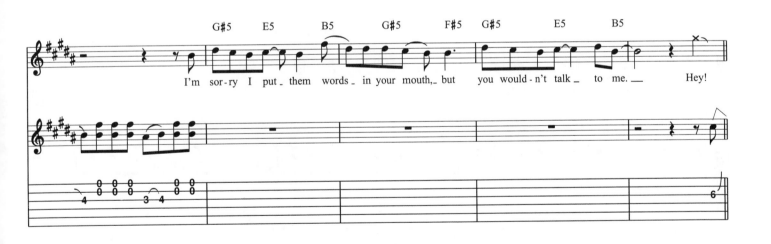

I'm sor - ry I put __ them words __ in your mouth, __ but you would - n't talk __ to me. __ Hey!

Guitar Solo

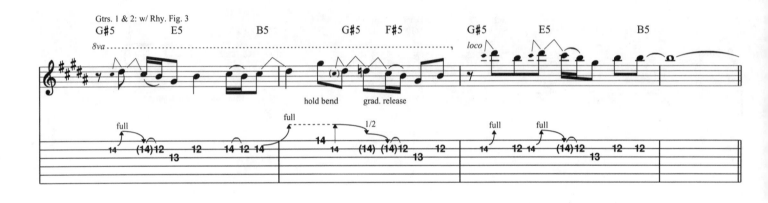

Bridge

You're ev-'ry-thing, __ I wan - na have __ a try. __   I'm

*Chord symbols reflect combined tonality.
**Riff A1 applies to Gtr. 2 only.

Coda

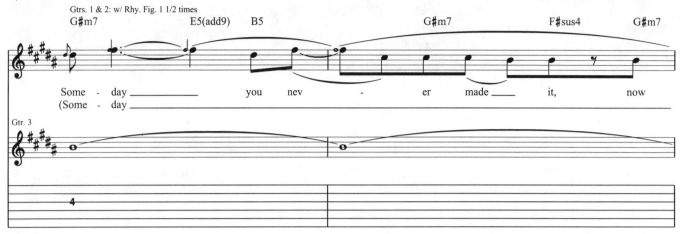

Some - day _____ you nev - - er made __ it, now
(Some - day _____

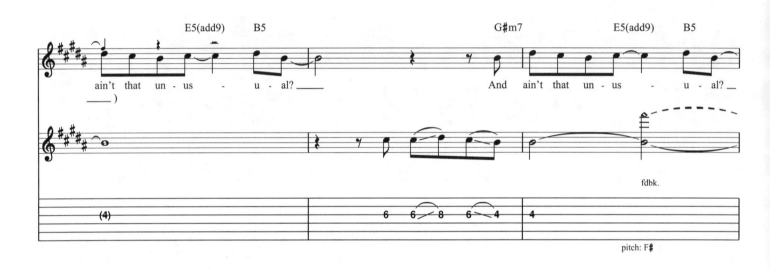

ain't that un - us - - u - al? ____ And ain't that un - us - - u - al?
____)

fdbk.

pitch: F♯

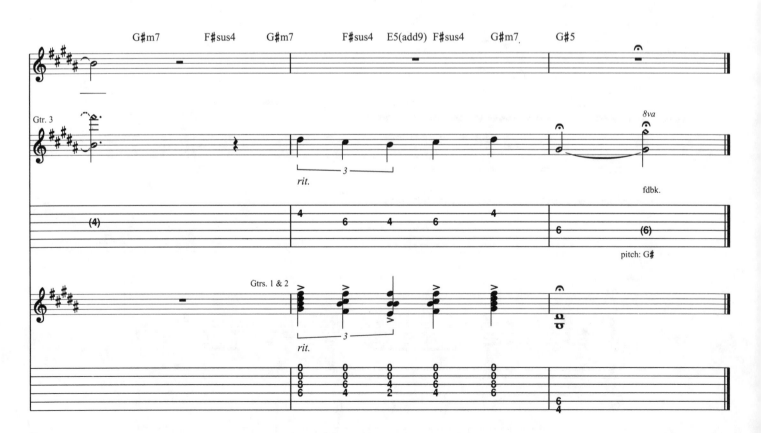

rit.

fdbk.

pitch: G♯

rit.

So Long

Words and Music by Goo Goo Dolls

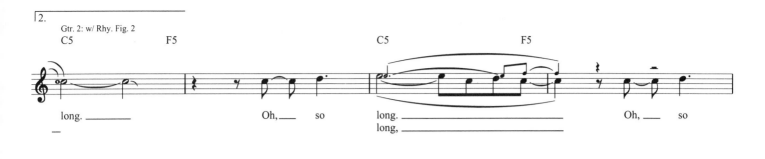

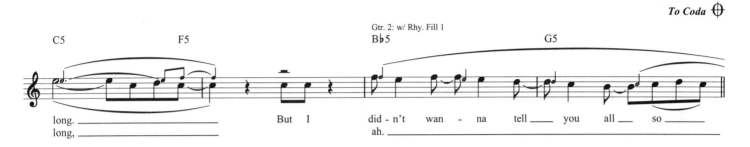

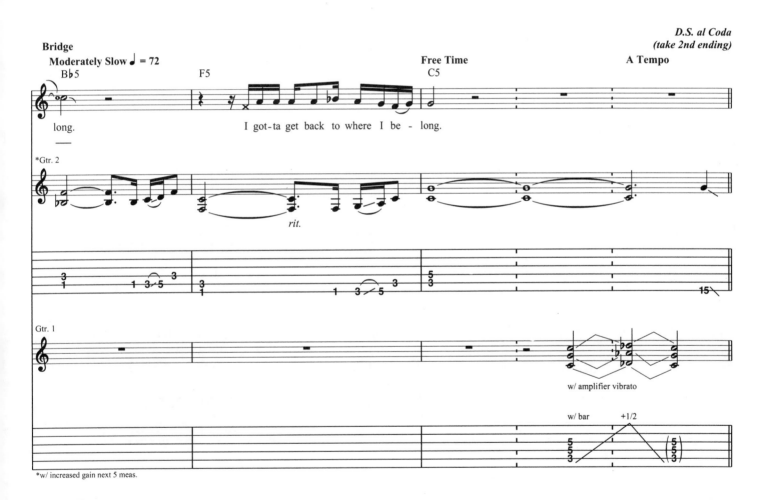

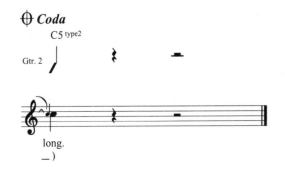

Eyes Wide Open

Words and Music by Goo Goo Dolls

Verse

for - tun - ate son __ of a for - tun - ate son. __ The Liv - ing large __ on the wrong __ side of town. __
don't take the bus __ and I nev - er walk too far. __ The furth - est I got __ was my own __ back - yard. __ With a

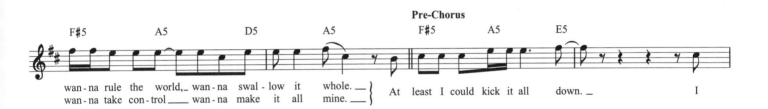

Too man - y friends __ and the fun __ nev - er ends, __ drink - in' and hang - in' a - round. __ I
fist - ful of cash __ that some - bod - y else earned, __ send me some more __ when it all __ got burned. __ I

Pre-Chorus

wan - na rule the world, __ wan - na swal - low it whole. __ } At least I could kick it all down. __ I
wan - na take con - trol __ wan - na make it all mine. __ }

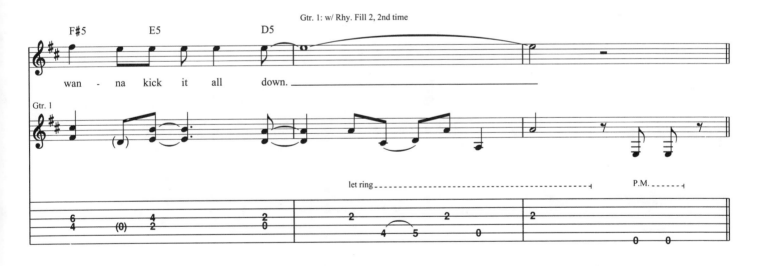

wan - na kick it all down. ____

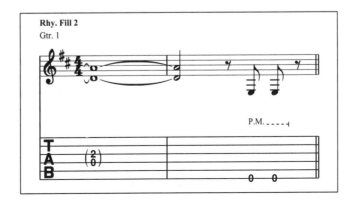

Eyes wide o - pen, I ___ can't see. ___ Eyes wide o - pen, what ___

___ you mean. ___ Eyes wide o - pen, I ___ can't seem ___ to be. ___

___ My eyes wide o - pen, I ___

___ can't see. ___ Eyes wide o - pen, what ___ you mean. ___

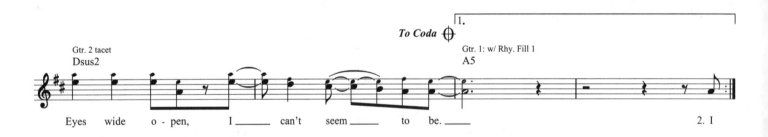

Eyes wide o - pen, I ___ can't seem ___ to be. ___ 2. I

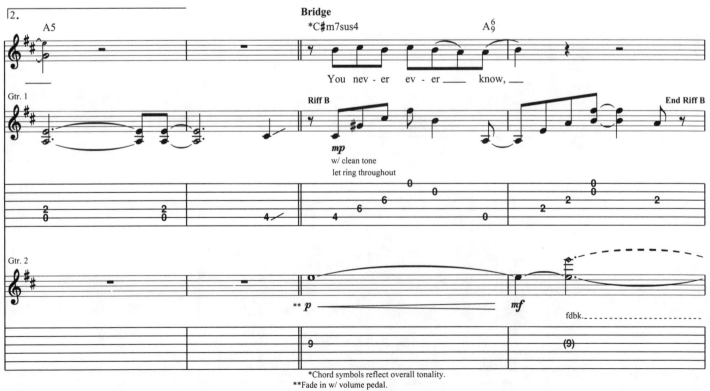

You nev - er ev - er ___ know, ___

*Chord symbols reflect overall tonality.
**Fade in w/ volume pedal.

78

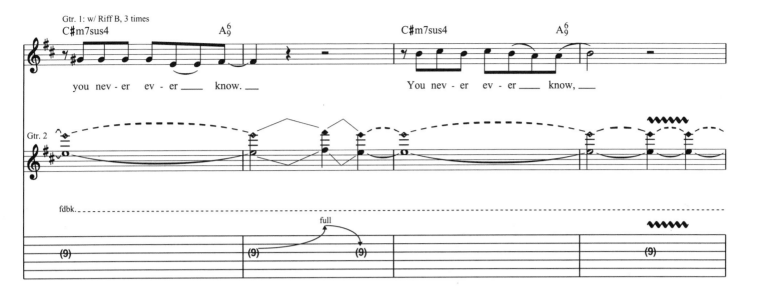

Gtr. 1: w/ Riff B, 3 times

C#m7sus4   A9^6   C#m7sus4   A9^6

you nev - er ev - er ___ know. ___   You nev - er ev - er ___ know, ___

Gtr. 2

fdbk.

Interlude

C#m7sus4   A9^6   D5   E5   F#5   E5

you nev - er ev - er ___ know. ___

Gtr. 2

fdbk.

Gtr. 3 (dist.)

8va   *loco*

pp ___ *f*

fdbk.

pitch: C

Gtr. 1

f w/ dist.

*Fade in w/ volume pedal.

Guitar Solo

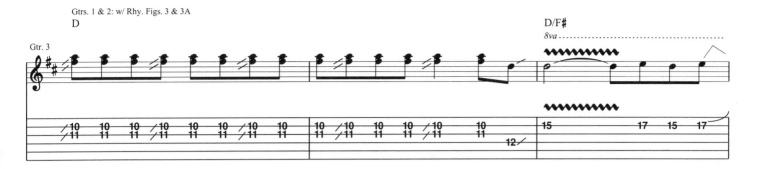

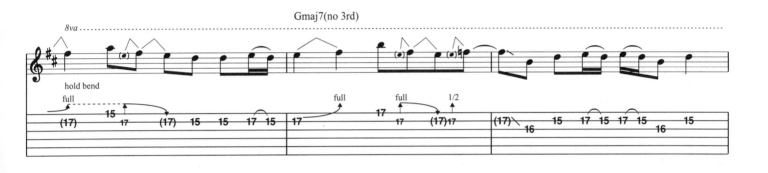

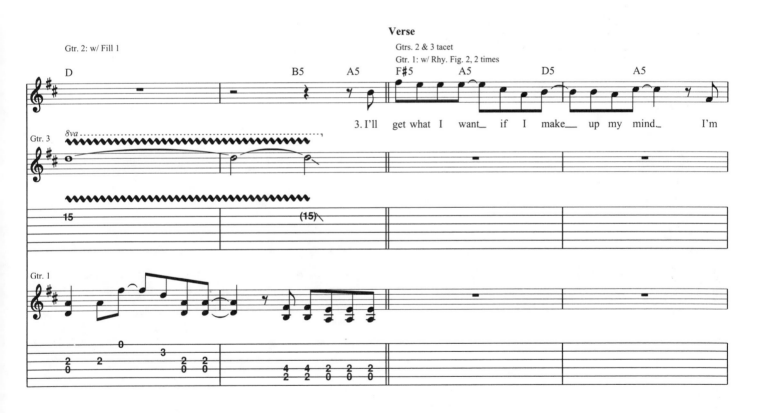

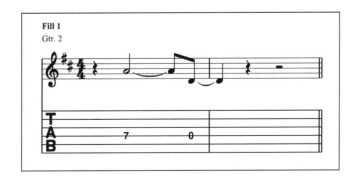

turn - in' you in - side ___ out. ___   I wan-na rule the world, _ wan-na swal -

Pre-Chorus

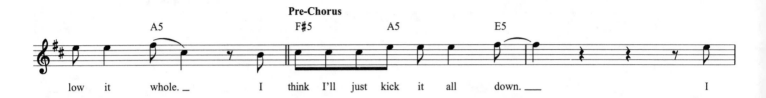

low it whole. _   I think I'll just kick it all down. ___   I

D.S. al Coda

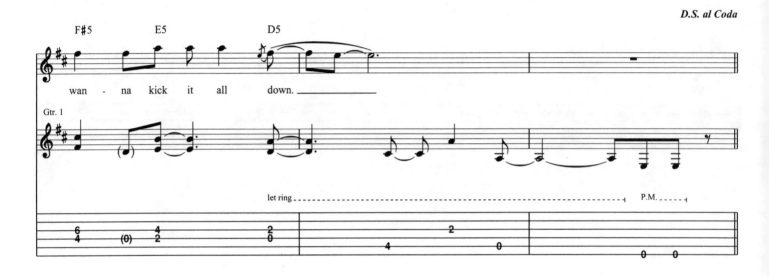

wan - na kick it all down. ___

Gtr. 1

let ring -⌐ P.M. - - - -⌐

Coda

Gtr. 1: w/ Rhy. Fig. 1, last 2 meas.

A5

Gtr. 2: w/ Fill 3

Outro

Begin Fade

Gtr. 1: w/ Rhy. Fig. 1

Dsus2   D/F#   Dsus2/A

Eyes wide o - pen.   Eyes wide o - pen.

Repeat and Fade

Gtr. 2: w/ Riff A, 1st time

Dsus2   A5

Eyes wide o - pen.

Fill 3
Gtr. 2

Disconnected

By Joe Bompczyk, Bob Guariglia, Pete Secrist and Fred Suchman

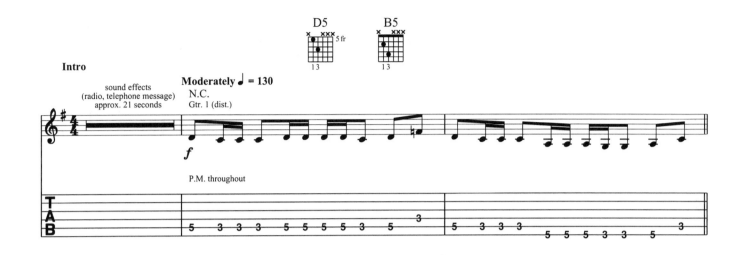

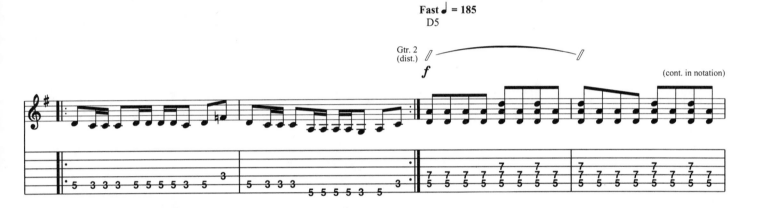

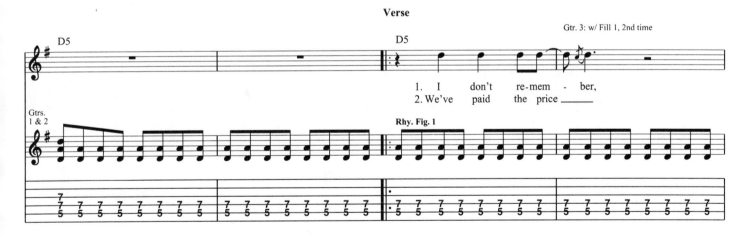

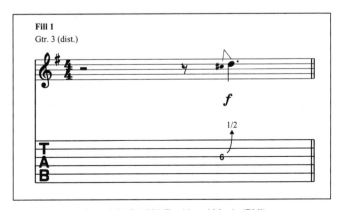

Oh, you're so ___ dis - tant, noth - in's come a - long. ___ Yeah.

End Rhy. Fig. 2

Interlude

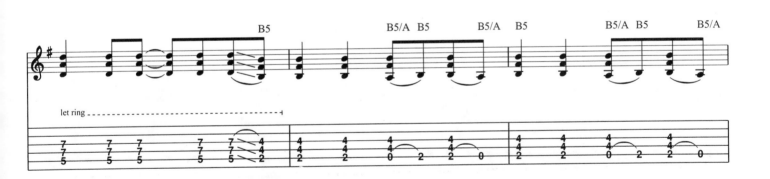

1.

2.

D.S. al Coda

'Cause

⊕ *Coda*

I've been dis - con - nect - ed, some - one pulled the plug. __

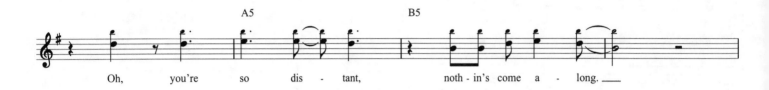

Oh, you're so dis - tant, noth - in's come a - long. __

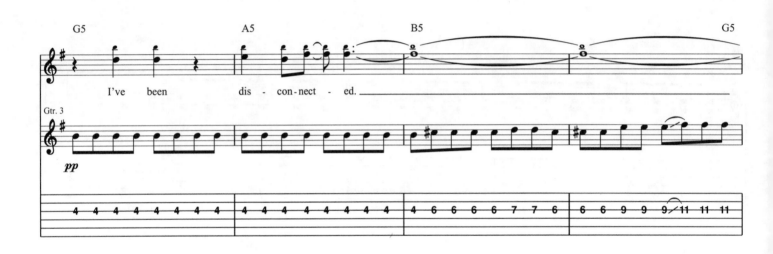

I've been dis - con - nect - ed. _____

Outro

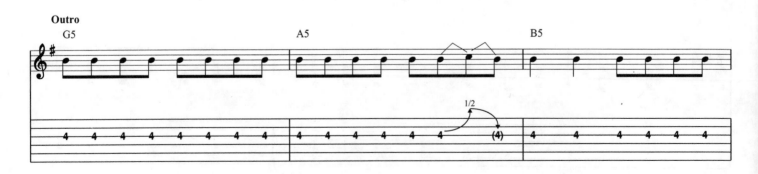

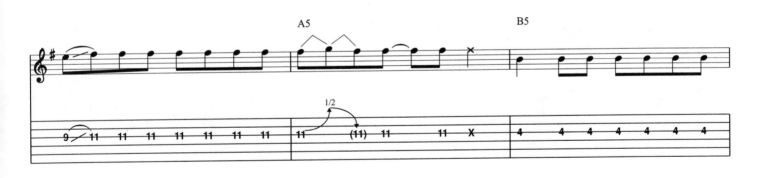

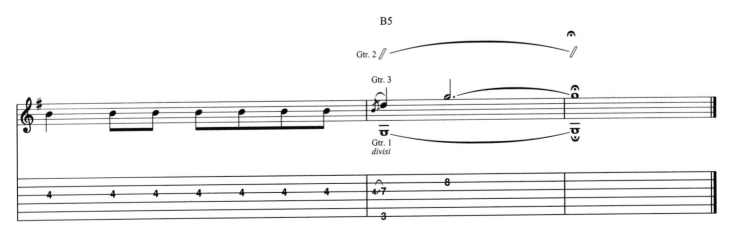

Slave Girl

By M. Blood and R. Jakimyszyn

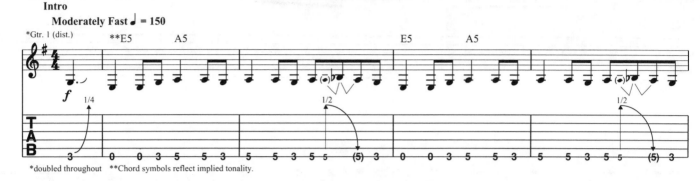

*doubled throughout   **Chord symbols reflect implied tonality.

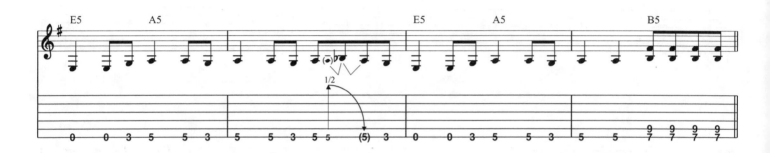

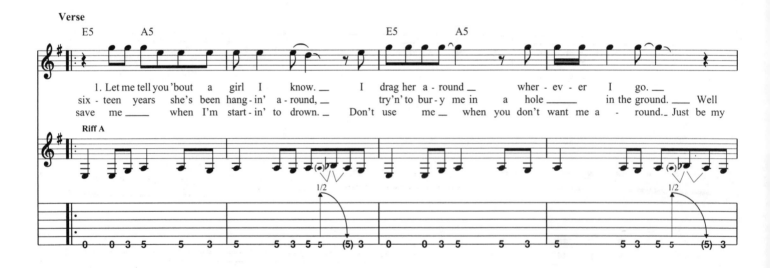

1. Let me tell you 'bout a girl I know. ___ I drag her a-round ___ wher-ev-er I go. ___
six-teen years she's been hang-in' a-round, ___ try'n' to bur-y me in a hole ___ in the ground. ___ Well
save me ___ when I'm start-in' to drown. ___ Don't use me ___ when you don't want me a-round. ___ Just be my

This lit-tle wo-man drives ___ me in-sane. ___ She's tied to my an-kle with a ball and chain. ___ 2. For
I think it's time that I e-ven the score. ___ There's
slave girl ___ 'cause that's all I need. ___ So

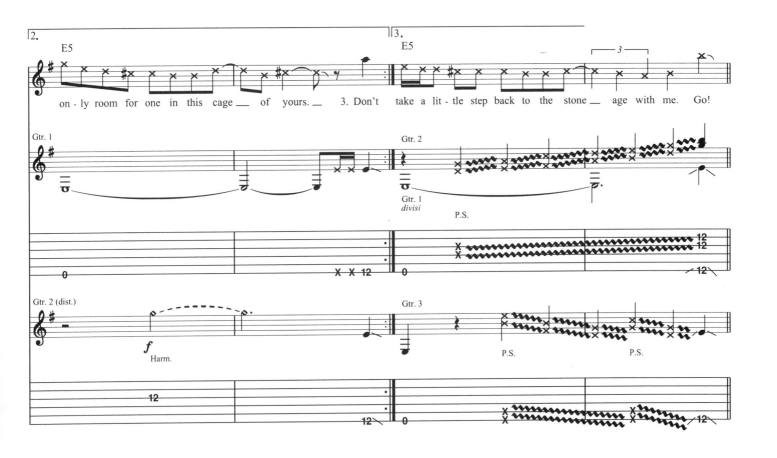

on-ly room for one in this cage___ of yours.___ 3. Don't take a lit-tle step back to the stone___ age with me. Go!

Guitar Solo

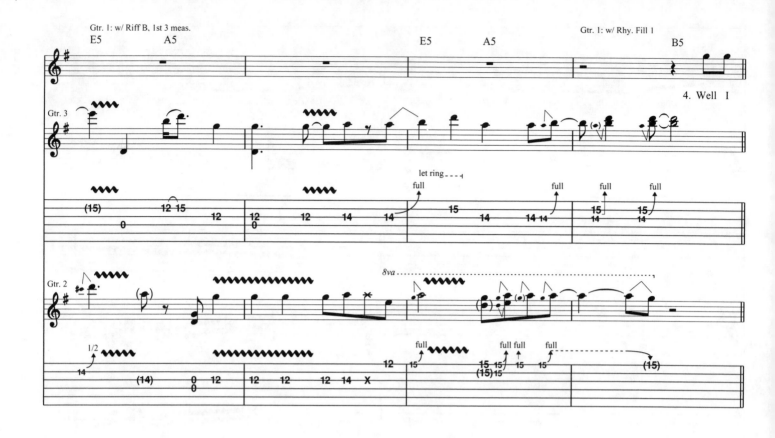

Verse

Gtrs. 2 & 3 tacet
Gtr. 1: w/ Riff A

E5   A5   E5   A5

hear a strange noise as I lie in my bed. ___ I feel a lot-ta wat-er drip-pin'
moved me when I was tak-in' my time. You a-bused me when I'm

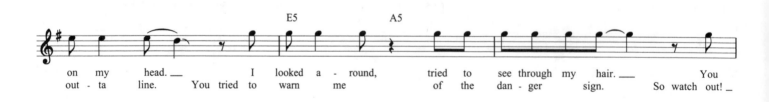

E5   A5

on my head. ___ I looked a-round, tried to see through my hair. ___ You
out-ta line. You tried to warn me of the dan-ger sign. So watch out! ___

1.

E5

left me a-lone, ___ but do you think I care? ___ 5. 'Cause you

Rhy. Fill 1
Gtr. 1

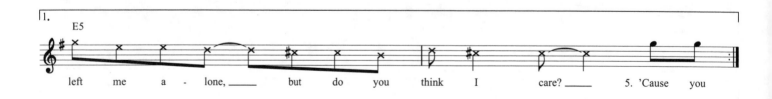

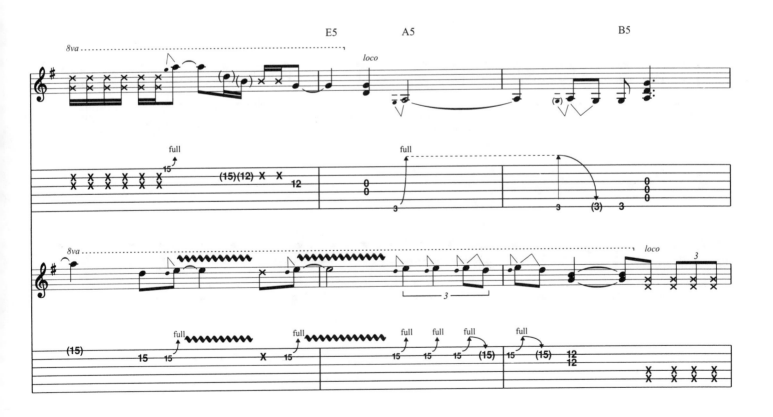

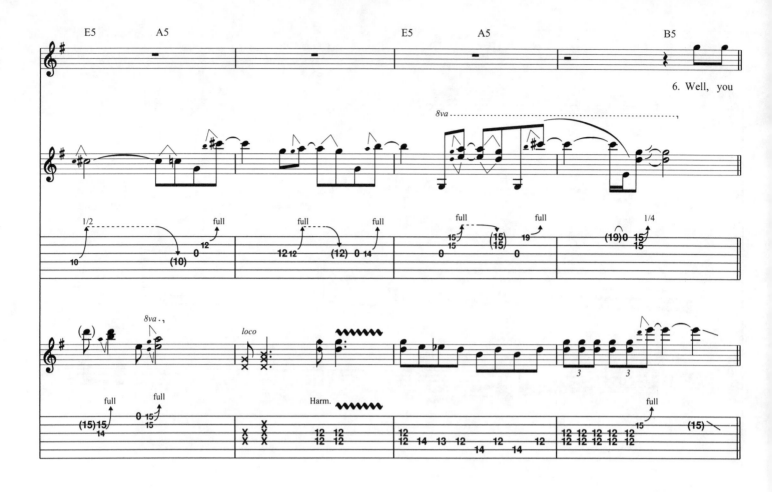

6. Well, you

Verse

Gtrs. 2 & 3 tacet
Gtr. 1: w/ Riff A, 1st time
Gtr. 1: w/ Riff A, 1st 6 meas., 2nd time

E5   A5   E5   A5

got me in the bond-age of an-oth-er age,___ you drive me to dis-trac-tion in a
chain gang,___ play a-long with me. I'll be your cave-man, it's bas-ic

E5   A5

prim-i-tive way.___ I can't con-trol my in-stincts when I hear her say,___ "Just
as can be. I'm not in-sane, man,___ I'm just out-ta my dream.___

come a-round and see me if you lose ___ your way." ___ 7. So join my

*Sung behind the beat.

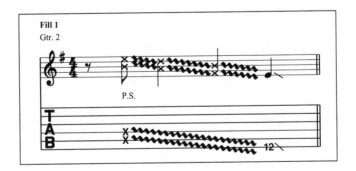

Fill 1
Gtr. 2

Guitar Notation Legend

Guitar Music can be notated three different ways: on a *musical staff*, in *tablature*, and in *rhythm slashes*.

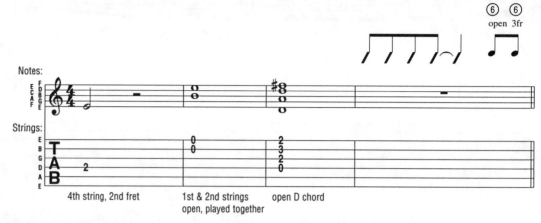

RHYTHM SLASHES are written above the staff. Strum chords in the rhythm indicated. Use the chord diagrams found at the top of the first page of the transcription for the appropriate chord voicings. Round noteheads indicate single notes.

THE MUSICAL STAFF shows pitches and rhythms and is divided by bar lines into measures. Pitches are named after the first seven letters of the alphabet.

TABLATURE graphically represents the guitar fingerboard. Each horizontal line represents a a string, and each number represents a fret.

4th string, 2nd fret

1st & 2nd strings open, played together

open D chord

Definitions for Special Guitar Notation

HALF-STEP BEND: Strike the note and bend up 1/2 step.

WHOLE-STEP BEND: Strike the note and bend up one step.

GRACE NOTE BEND: Strike the note and bend up as indicated. The first note does not take up any time.

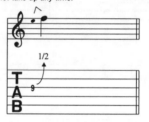

SLIGHT (MICROTONE) BEND: Strike the note and bend up 1/4 step.

BEND AND RELEASE: Strike the note and bend up as indicated, then release back to the original note. Only the first note is struck.

PRE-BEND: Bend the note as indicated, then strike it.

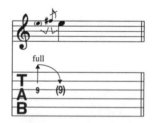

PRE-BEND AND RELEASE: Bend the note as indicated. Strike it and release the bend back to the original note.

UNISON BEND: Strike the two notes simultaneously and bend the lower note up to the pitch of the higher.

VIBRATO: The string is vibrated by rapidly bending and releasing the note with the fretting hand.

WIDE VIBRATO: The pitch is varied to a greater degree by vibrating with the fretting hand.

HAMMER-ON: Strike the first (lower) note with one finger, then sound the higher note (on the same string) with another finger by fretting it without picking.

PULL-OFF: Place both fingers on the notes to be sounded. Strike the first note and without picking, pull the finger off to sound the second (lower) note.

LEGATO SLIDE: Strike the first note and then slide the same fret-hand finger up or down to the second note. The second note is not struck.

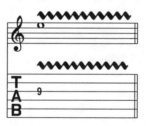

SHIFT SLIDE: Same as legato slide, except the second note is struck.

TRILL: Very rapidly alternate between the notes indicated by continuously hammering on and pulling off.

TAPPING: Hammer ("tap") the fret indicated with the pick-hand index or middle finger and pull off to the note fretted by the fret hand.

NATURAL HARMONIC: Strike the note while the fret-hand lightly touches the string directly over the fret indicated.

PINCH HARMONIC: The note is fretted normally and a harmonic is produced by adding the edge of the thumb or the tip of the index finger of the pick hand to the normal pick attack.

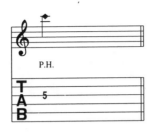

HARP HARMONIC: The note is fretted normally and a harmonic is produced by gently resting the pick hand's index finger directly above the indicated fret (in parentheses) while the pick hand's thumb or pick assists by plucking the appropriate string.

PICK SCRAPE: The edge of the pick is rubbed down (or up) the string, producing a scratchy sound.

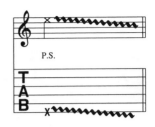

MUFFLED STRINGS: A percussive sound is produced by laying the fret hand across the string(s) without depressing, and striking them with the pick hand.

PALM MUTING: The note is partially muted by the pick hand lightly touching the string(s) just before the bridge.

RAKE: Drag the pick across the strings indicated with a single motion.

TREMOLO PICKING: The note is picked as rapidly and continuously as possible.

ARPEGGIATE: Play the notes of the chord indicated by quickly rolling them from bottom to top.

VIBRATO BAR DIVE AND RETURN: The pitch of the note or chord is dropped a specified number of steps (in rhythm) then returned to the original pitch.

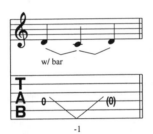

VIBRATO BAR SCOOP: Depress the bar just before striking the note, then quickly release the bar.

VIBRATO BAR DIP: Strike the note and then immediately drop a specified number of steps, then release back to the original pitch.

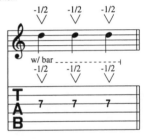

Additional Musical Definitions

  (accent) • Accentuate note (play it louder)

  (accent) • Accentuate note with great intensity

(staccato) • Play the note short

⊓ • Downstroke

∨ • Upstroke

D.S. al Coda • Go back to the sign (𝄋), then play until the measure marked "**To Coda**," then skip to the section labelled "**Coda**."

D.S. al Fine • Go back to the beginning of the song and play until the measure marked "**Fine**" (end).

Rhy. Fig. • Label used to recall a recurring accompaniment pattern (usually chordal).

Riff • Label used to recall composed, melodic lines (usually single notes) which recur.

Fill • Label used to identify a brief melodic figure which is to be inserted into the arrangement.

Rhy. Fill • A chordal version of a Fill.

tacet • Instrument is silent (drops out).

 • Repeat measures between signs.

| 1. | 2. | • When a repeated section has different endings, play the first ending only the first time and the second ending only the second time.

NOTE: Tablature numbers in parentheses mean:
1. The note is being sustained over a system (note in standard notation is tied), or
2. The note is sustained, but a new articulation (such as a hammer-on, pull-off, slide or vibrato begins, or
3. The note is a barely audible "ghost" note (note in standard notation is also in parentheses).

RECORDED VERSIONS
The Best Note-For-Note Transcriptions Available

RECORDED VERSIONS GUITAR

ALL BOOKS INCLUDE TABLATURE

00690002 Aerosmith – Big Ones	$22.95	
00694909 Aerosmith – Get A Grip	$19.95	
00692015 Aerosmith's Greatest Hits	$19.95	
00660133 Aerosmith – Pump	$19.95	
00694865 Alice In Chains – Dirt	$19.95	
00660225 Alice In Chains – Facelift	$19.95	
00694925 Alice In Chains – Jar Of Flies/Sap	$19.95	
00694932 Allman Brothers Band – Vol. 1	$24.95	
00694933 Allman Brothers Band – Vol. 2	$24.95	
00694934 Allman Brothers Band – Vol. 3	$24.95	
00694826 Anthrax – Attack Of The Killer B's	$19.95	
00694876 Chet Atkins – Contemporary Styles	$19.95	
00694877 Chet Atkins – Guitar For All Seasons	$19.95	
00694918 The Randy Bachman Collection	$22.95	
00694929 Beatles: 1962-1966	$24.95	
00694930 Beatles: 1967-1970	$24.95	
00694880 Beatles – Abbey Road	$19.95	
00694832 Beatles For Acoustic Guitar	$19.95	
00660140 Beatles Guitar Book	$19.95	
00690044 Beatles – Live At The BBC	$22.95	
00694891 Beatles – Revolver	$19.95	
00694914 Beatles – Rubber Soul	$19.95	
00694863 Beatles – Sgt. Pepper's Lonely Hearts Club Band	$19.95	
00694931 Belly – Star	$19.95	
00694884 The Best of George Benson	$19.95	
00692385 Chuck Berry	$19.95	
00692200 Black Sabbath – We Sold Our Soul For Rock 'N' Roll	$19.95	
00694770 Jon Bon Jovi – Blaze Of Glory	$19.95	
00690008 Bon Jovi – Cross Road	$19.95	
00694871 Bon Jovi – Keep The Faith	$19.95	
00694775 Bon Jovi – Slippery When Wet	$19.95	
00690102 Bon Jovi – These Days	$19.95	
00694935 Boston: Double Shot Of Boston	$22.95	
00694762 Cinderella – Heartbreak Station	$19.95	
00692376 Cinderella – Long Cold Winter	$19.95	
00692375 Cinderella – Night Songs	$19.95	
00694875 Eric Clapton – Boxed Set	$75.00	
00692392 Eric Clapton – Crossroads Vol. 1	$22.95	
00692393 Eric Clapton – Crossroads Vol. 2	$22.95	
00692394 Eric Clapton – Crossroads Vol. 3	$22.95	
00690010 Eric Clapton – From The Cradle	$19.95	
00660139 Eric Clapton – Journeyman	$19.95	
00694869 Eric Clapton – Unplugged	$19.95	
00692391 The Best of Eric Clapton	$19.95	
00694896 John Mayall/Eric Clapton – Bluesbreakers	$19.95	
00694873 Eric Clapton – Timepieces	$19.95	
00694837 Albert Collins – The Complete Imperial Recordings	$19.95	
00694862 Contemporary Country Guitar	$18.95	
00660127 Alice Cooper – Trash	$19.95	
00694941 Crash Test Dummies – God Shuffled His Feet	$19.95	
00694840 Cream – Disraeli Gears	$19.95	
00690007 Danzig 4	$19.95	
00694844 Def Leppard – Adrenalize	$19.95	
00660186 Alex De Grassi Guitar Collection	$19.95	
00694831 Derek And The Dominos – Layla & Other Assorted Love Songs	$19.95	
00660175 Dio – Lock Up The Wolves	$19.95	
00660178 Willie Dixon	$24.95	
00694920 Best of Free	$18.95	
00690089 Foo Fighters	$19.95	
00690042 Robben Ford Blues Collection	$19.95	
00694894 Frank Gambale – The Great Explorers	$19.95	
00694807 Danny Gatton – 88 Elmira St	$19.95	
00694848 Genuine Rockabilly Guitar Hits	$19.95	

00694798 George Harrison Anthology	$19.95	
00690068 Return of The Hellecasters	$19.95	
00692930 Jimi Hendrix – Are You Experienced?	$19.95	
00692931 Jimi Hendrix – Axis: Bold As Love	$19.95	
00694944 Jimi Hendrix – Blues	$24.95	
00660192 The Jimi Hendrix – Concerts	$24.95	
00692932 Jimi Hendrix – Electric Ladyland	$24.95	
00694923 Jimi Hendrix – The Experience Collection Boxed Set	$75.00	
00660099 Jimi Hendrix – Radio One	$24.95	
00694919 Jimi Hendrix – Stone Free	$19.95	
00660024 Jimi Hendrix – Variations On A Theme: Red House	$19.95	
00690017 Jimi Hendrix – Woodstock	$24.95	
00690038 Gary Hoey – Best Of	$19.95	
00660029 Buddy Holly	$19.95	
00660200 John Lee Hooker – The Healer	$19.95	
00660169 John Lee Hooker – A Blues Legend	$19.95	
00690054 Hootie & The Blowfish – Cracked Rear View	$19.95	
00694905 Howlin' Wolf	$14.95	
00694850 Iron Maiden – Fear Of The Dark	$19.95	
00694938 Elmore James – Master Electric Slide Guitar	$14.95	
00694833 Billy Joel For Guitar	$19.95	
00660147 Eric Johnson	$19.95	
00694912 Eric Johnson – Ah Via Musicom	$19.95	
00694911 Eric Johnson – Tones	$19.95	
00694799 Robert Johnson – At The Crossroads	$19.95	
00693185 Judas Priest – Vintage Hits	$19.95	
00660050 B. B. King	$19.95	
00690019 King's X – Best Of	$19.95	
00694903 The Best Of Kiss	$24.95	
00690070 Live – Throwing Copper	$19.95	
00694954 Lynyrd Skynyrd, New Best Of	$19.95	
00694845 Yngwie Malmsteen – Fire And Ice	$19.95	
00694756 Yngwie Malmsteen – Marching Out	$19.95	
00694755 Yngwie Malmsteen's Rising Force	$19.95	
00660001 Yngwie Malmsteen's Rising Force – Odyssey	$19.95	
00694757 Yngwie Malmsteen – Trilogy	$19.95	
00694956 Bob Marley – Legend	$19.95	
00690075 Bob Marley – Natural Mystic	$19.95	
00694945 Bob Marley – Songs Of Freedom	$24.95	
00690020 Meat Loaf – Bat Out Of Hell I & II	$22.95	
00694952 Megadeth – Countdown To Extinction	$19.95	
00694951 Megadeth – Rust In Peace	$22.95	
00694953 Megadeth – Selections From "Peace Sells... But Who's Buying?" & "So Far, So Good...So What!"	$22.95	
00690011 Megadeath – Youthanasia	$19.95	
00694868 Gary Moore – After Hours	$19.95	
00694849 Gary Moore – The Early Years	$19.95	
00694802 Gary Moore – Still Got The Blues	$19.95	
00690103 Alanis Morissette – Jagged Little Pill	$19.95	
00694958 Mountain, Best Of	$19.95	
00694895 Nirvana – Bleach	$19.95	
00694913 Nirvana – In Utero	$19.95	
00694901 Nirvana – Incesticide	$19.95	
00694883 Nirvana – Nevermind	$19.95	
00690026 Nirvana – Unplugged In New York	$19.95	
00694847 Best Of Ozzy Osbourne	$22.95	
00694830 Ozzy Osbourne – No More Tears	$19.95	
00694855 Pearl Jam – Ten	$19.95	
00693800 Pink Floyd – Early Classics	$19.95	
00693864 Police, The Best Of	$18.95	
00694967 Police – Message In A Box Boxed Set	$70.00	
00692535 Elvis Presley	$18.95	
00690032 Elvis Presley – The Sun Sessions	$22.95	
00694975 Queen – Classic	$24.95	

00694974 Queen – A Night At The Opera	$19.95	
00694969 Queensryche – Selections from "Operation: Mindcrime"	$19.95	
00694910 Rage Against The Machine	$19.95	
00693910 Ratt – Invasion of Your Privacy	$19.95	
00693911 Ratt – Out Of The Cellar	$19.95	
00690055 Red Hot Chili Peppers – Bloodsugarsexmagik	$19.95	
00690090 Red Hot Chili Peppers – One Hot Minute	$22.95	
00690027 Red Hot Chili Peppers – Out In L.A.	$19.95	
00694968 Red Hot Chili Peppers – Selections from "What Hits!?"	$22.95	
00694892 Guitar Style Of Jerry Reed	$19.95	
00694899 REM – Automatic For The People	$19.95	
00694898 REM – Out Of Time	$19.95	
00660060 Robbie Robertson	$19.95	
00694959 Rockin' Country Guitar	$19.95	
00690014 Rolling Stones – Exile On Main Street	$24.95	
00694976 Rolling Stones – Some Girls	$18.95	
00694897 Roots Of Country Guitar	$19.95	
00694836 Richie Sambora – Stranger In This Town	$19.95	
00694805 Scorpions – Crazy World	$19.95	
00694916 Scorpions – Face The Heat	$19.95	
00694870 Seattle Scene	$18.95	
00690076 Sex Pistols – Never The Bollocks, Here's The Sex Pistols	$19.95	
00690041 Smithereens – Best Of	$19.95	
00694885 Spin Doctors – Pocket Full Of Kryptonite	$19.95	
00694962 Spin Doctors – Turn It Upside Down	$19.95	
00694917 Spin Doctors – Up For Grabs	$19.95	
00694921 Steppenwolf, The Best Of	$22.95	
00694801 Rod Stewart, Best Of	$22.95	
00694957 Rod Stewart – Unplugged...And Seated	$22.95	
00690021 Sting – Fields Of Gold	$19.95	
00694824 Best Of James Taylor	$16.95	
00694846 Testament – The Ritual	$19.95	
00694887 Thin Lizzy – The Best Of Thin Lizzy	$19.95	
00690030 Toad The Wet Sprocket	$19.95	
00694410 The Best of U2	$19.95	
00694411 U2 – The Joshua Tree	$19.95	
00690039 Steve Vai – Alien Love Secrets	$24.95	
00660137 Steve Vai – Passion & Warfare	$24.95	
00694904 Vai – Sex and Religion	$24.95	
00690023 Jimmy Vaughan – Strange Pleasures	$19.95	
00690024 Stevie Ray Vaughan – Couldn't Stand The Weather	$19.95	
00694879 Stevie Ray Vaughan – In The Beginning	$19.95	
00660136 Stevie Ray Vaughan – In Step	$19.95	
00660058 Stevie Ray Vaughan – Lightnin' Blues 1983 – 1987	$24.95	
00690036 Stevie Ray Vaughan – Live Alive	$24.95	
00694835 Stevie Ray Vaughan – The Sky Is Crying	$19.95	
00690015 Stevie Ray Vaughan – Texas Flood	$19.95	
00690025 Stevie Ray Vaughan – Soul To Soul	$19.95	
00694776 Vaughan Brothers – Family Style	$19.95	
00660196 Vixen – Rev It Up	$19.95	
00694844 Muddy Waters – Deep Blues	$24.95	
00690071 Weezer		
00694888 Windham Hill Guitar Sampler	$18.95	

Prices and availability subject to change without notice.
Some products may not be available outside the U.S.A.

FOR MORE INFORMATION, SEE YOUR LOCAL MUSIC DEALER,
OR WRITE TO:

HAL•LEONARD

0196